CW01272323

CHAMPERS

The Kid That Did

Shane J. Lloyd

authorHOUSE

AuthorHouse™ UK Ltd.
500 Avebury Boulevard
Central Milton Keynes, MK9 2BE
www.authorhouse.co.uk
Phone: 08001974150

© 2009 Shane J. Lloyd. All rights reserved.

No part of this book may be reproduced, stored in a retrieval system, or transmitted by any means without the written permission of the author.

First published by AuthorHouse 10/12/2009

ISBN: 978-1-4389-5853-8 (sc)

This book is printed on acid-free paper.

About Champers

    This is the true life experience of a colourful character who was blamed for kidnapping a member of the Brit Boy Band 'East 17' back in 1999, Showered completely naked with all five 'Spice Girls,' Partied with porn stars Linzie Dawn Mackenzie and Suzie Wilden on a wild night out in Tenerife, Drank cocktails with S Club 7s sexy Rachel, Went on an all night bender with comic Lenny Henry, and befriended the World Heavyweight Boxing Champion 'Big Frank Bruno.'
    His name is 'Champers' we think you'll like him................

Acknowledgements

    I would like to say a 'Big Thanks' to all of the people who have been or, who still are a part of my life and made it possible for me to tell this story. To the people who helped and supported me when the going got tuff and a 'Very Special Thanks' to my good friend Steve Pettitt for his constant trips across the water and help when I needed it most!

"Buckle up your seatbelts!"

CONTENTS

About Champers	V
Acknowledgements	Vii
Here Comes Trouble	1
What Do I Do Now?	3
Welcome To Party World	6
Banged Up Abroad	14
Tenerife Ii	16
Drugs Mugs And Thugs	20
Meet The Boys	35
The Bigger The 'Up' The Bigger The 'Down'	44
Fetch The Coppers	45
C.P. Tenerife Ii	50
No Bail Just Jail	54
Butlins '97'	55
Why Are We Waiting?	114
Tenerife Uncovered	116
Royal Judge Baltazar Garzon	135
Sort It Out!	141
The Call	143
Ernie	145
Solvent Abuse	149
"I'm A Celebrity Get Me Out Of Here!"	151

Fantasy Island	154
Are You LOnesome Tonight?	157
The Knocking Shop	159
Senor Bond	164
Tortured	171
The Big Fight	175
11:09pm	190
It's All Gone Pete Tong	194
The Day Before Judgement Day	199
Judgement Day	200
Shouts	204
Tenerife	207
About The Author	209

HERE COMES TROUBLE

I was delivered at the Manor hospital in Walsall, West Midlands, the son of Doreen and John. Times were hard in those days and I spent the first few years of my life in Caldmore, which was one of the rougher parts of the West Midlands and still is to this very day.

My farther pulled the boards off a condemned house which was due for demolition to provide a house for the family to be, and stole and borrowed items of furniture, beds and sofas to furnish the home as money at the time was hard to come by.

We later moved to Harden, which was closer to the families of my mother, and this is where we stayed for some years.

I was in my 16th year and my younger brother who was 4 years my junior had just turned 12. The past 3 years hadn't been a good spell as my father had suffered from cancer twice and hepatitis. The latter wasn't helped by the amount of booze he used to sink, and trust me, Johnny Lloyd could drink!

I can remember every time I used to pass the Welcome Stranger pub, my dad's local. They had frosted glass windows the sort you can just see silhouettes and colours through. There was a windowsill full of Guinness bottles where he used to sit all night chatting about pigeons and the normal things you gas about when having a good session with the lads. My mother was a beautiful woman and everyone I knew complimented her on her looks and politeness as she never had a bad word to say about anyone. She was the one who was always motivated to earn money, setting up her own businesses and such to help pay the bills. Many times I'd have my friends question me over the nice looking girl who'd dropped me off outside their houses, and I had to explain it was my mother and to tread careful with any further remarks.

I also had another brother Paul who was from a previous marriage of my mothers, but we grew up as proper brothers nevertheless and were all as one.

After nursing my father through his numerous bouts of throat and nasal cancer he finally was diagnosed clear from it all.

It must have only been 2 to 3 weeks when my mother took ill.

She was only a dainty lady weighing 8 stone 7lbs at a height of 5 feet 2 inches. Within 7 days she had ballooned to 12 stones most of which was water retention. The doctor had prescribed diuretics, but as the days went on it became more and more serious. The ambulance came and she was rushed into hospital.

Being 16 years old is one of those ages when your hormones are all starting to kick into high gear. You're changing from a little boy into a man, suffering from acne and the whole life thing is a ball of confusion. You need guiding and are absorbing information from all around. Anything you take in is, for sure, to affect you for a very long time in your future life.

I went with my father and my two brothers to the Manor hospital to see how my mom was doing with the mysterious illness which had taken her. She looked very calm and relaxed.

I can still picture her even 20 years on, with a small drip in her arm and a pretty little smile on her face when we greeted her. We all chatted for an hour or so and did the usual things you do when trying to lift the spirits of someone in hospital. It seemed really strange that only two months earlier it was my father in the bed, with my mother by the side. I just couldn't work it out. It was time to go. The nurse came and told us and we all said our goodbyes. I leant over the bed kissed my pretty mother on the lips and said "Bye-bye". It was the last time I would ever see her again.

The following day she passed away. My father woke us up in the morning and told us 'she'd gone.'

The tears flooded, and a rollercoaster of emotions surged through my already confused teenage mind.

"What do I do now?"

WHAT DO I DO NOW

Things changed in a big way. My outlook on life changed radically.

"Fuck everybody!" was my motto.

I started to work at a Sports car garage called 'MG Motors' in Leamore, close to the family home. I'd always been car mad since I was a kid and completed a three year course in motor vehicle maintenance at West Bromwich College just outside of Walsall.

Ian and Bob, the two owners, were really nice blokes and we got on well. I stayed there for around two years and enjoyed the work I did. The problem was that when your seventeen and being paid by the government on YTS training schemes, you grafted 6 days a week, 50 hours a week and only got paid 26 pounds. Ian and Bob used to compensate a little by giving me a 'Tenner' back hander and always commented on how tight the bastards were for not paying us any more!

"I needed more dollars!"

My older mates were all going out three nights a week, getting pissed and coming home with tales of all the 'dragons' they'd shagged. There I was, working my bollocks off and after paying out all of my weekly debts I had just enough money left to buy a can of coke and cigarettes for the rest of the week. Things needed to change 'rapid!'

I'd never really been in much trouble with the old bill whilst my mother was alive as I didn't want to upset her, and besides that my father would have killed me, although the one time, shortly after Christmas, I got nicked for shooting someone through the windows of the Co-op dairy.

My dad had bought me an air rifle as a Christmas present with telescopic night sights, and me, not being happy with cans and bottles, decided to take a few shots at 'live' targets. The coppers confiscated the gun and I had to appear in front of the Chief Inspector of Police, for an 'off the record' bollocking.

My parents were not amused!

I used to knock around with a kid, a good old mate of mine called 'Neil Craddock' or 'Crad' as we called him for short. Crad was a big strapping lad, always pissed and always up for a row. He fuckin loved it!

Flix night club in Bloxwich was a rough place at 2 am in the morning. You were guaranteed to find two or three pools of blood and a few teeth lying in the gutter every Sunday morning without fail.

We left about 1:30 ish, because the bouncer had chucked us out for 'apparently' abusing some birds. The prick had seen the girl smiling over in his direction and thought he was in with a chance, when later realising that she was having the 'two finger special from Champers up the bar he then threw a wobbly. The cunt gave me a black eye and cracked one of my ribs.

I later found out that they'd both started going out together and some weeks after, I shagged her then ever so politely dropped her off outside his house, Wet as a window cleaners leather!. Revenge is sweet!

We decided to do the usual thing pissed up people do on Saturday night after 15 pints of Tenants Extra and Diamond white Snakebites, 'The Kebab shop.' The Problem was we'd got no dough left. Crad, in the shuffle, had lost his last tenner. We were gutted.

'How the fuck are we going to get home?' I thought

"Let's nick a car." He said, in a slurred voice.

He looked over onto the Asda car park and sitting there was a bright yellow Escort with wide wheels and blacked out windows.

"Fuck me Crad, you can hardly stand up never mind drive you cunt," I informed him.

"Bollocks," He replied back, "I'm as sober as a judge."

We staggered over to the shiny pimp looking car then looked around to see if anyone was watching us. Crad decided to piss up the driver side back wheel whilst searching through his ripped jacket pocket for the rusty old escort key he kept on his key ring. The piss drenched his trousers as he leant into the side of the car. You'd be lying if you said that you had never been in a similar situation one time or another? Lying Bastard!

Fuck me, every Saturday night he'd do exactly the same thing and if you were next to him you'd get the blame for pissing on him or he'd piss on your shoes as well. That's Crad for ya!

After wiping down his piss soaked trousers and kicking his shoes, which had two pools of the night's session in them, he proceeded to try his key in the lock. "Look out Lloydy," he said, "The cop shop's over the road," he added.

We stood there for about an hour and finally he screamed. "I've got the fucker!" as he jumped inside and pushed the key into the ignition.

It fitted like a glove. The engine roared to life and big smiles like Cheshire cats were worn by both of us, but not for long.

We'd been there for so much time that the owner had seen us trying to rob his car and had run across the road to the Police station. Two panda cars and three Foot Patrol were flying across the car park towards us. We were so pissed we just fell out and landed on the floor either side of the car like something out of a Laurel and Hardy film. This was to be my first of many encounters with the boys in blue, and later that month we both received a one hundred and fifty pound fine for tampering with a motor vehicle, and a sixth month suspended sentence for taking and driving away.

WELCOME TO PARTY WORLD

In 1989 after recently splitting up with my girlfriend of two years, I saw an advert in the local newspaper reading

'Outgoing bar staff wanted for newly opening Fun pub in Walsall.'

I'd never worked behind a bar before, but needed something to occupy my night times as I had little money and my head was still on *tilt* from recently splitting up with my girlfriend.

The opening was in mid April on a Friday night, so before committing myself to the unknown, I thought that I'd go take a look for myself.

I got there at 9.30pm. The taxi had dropped me off right outside the door where there must have been at least 200 people already queuing to get in. There were lots of fit little birds in tight short miniskirts covered in glitter, clutching their bags and purses waiting to pay the till girl to enter , get pissed out of their brains ,throw up ,and pull a fellow if they were lucky enough to still be able to talk at the end of the night.

The building was a big pink and blue one with "The Dilke fun pub," jazzily sign written across the front, with advertisements for pound drinks, 2 for 1 and lots of special offers scattered everywhere and the punters were pointing at what they were about to get leathered on that night, and regret the next morning.

I walked to the front of the queue where two of the doormen were standing, checking out the talent and vetting some of the blokes who didn't realise that jeans and dirty trainers wasn't what they were looking for to enter into a newly opening establishment on Friday night.

"Excuse me," I said, trying to grab the attention of the taller one of the two, "I've come about the bar job."

"Hang on mate, I'll be with you in a minute," he replied, halfway through frisking two lads for any naughties they may have had on them.

A blue Ford Escort cabriolet pulled up close to the door and a doorman pointed a finger towards the driver.

"See him there mate, he'll sort you out."

The owner introduced himself as 'Graham' and I explained I'd come in response to his advert in the newspaper.

He took me inside past four other doormen who were greeting the thirsty punters eager to get to the bar, and showed me around.

There were eight 'fit' looking girls behind the bar dressed in cycling shorts and red and white rugby shirts, dancing, juggling bottles and throwing party streamers at the oncoming party goers in front of them.

It was quite big inside with a huge dance floor in the centre with six pillars surrounding it and lots of bay seating fixed to the back walls.

More and more people packed into the bubbling building until around 10:30pm it was absolutely chocker.

I'd already made up my mind. "When do I start?" I asked him.

The next night I got to work at 7:30pm and there were already a few of the bar staff sitting down supping diamond whites before their busy Saturday nights party.

Two doormen walked in, one about six feet three with slick back curly hair, This was Steve "Ice man" Pettitt, former Midland cruiser weight boxing champion .Proper bloke him and one of those people who you could count on your hand as being a 'real friend' and that's what he became to me as the years rolled on.

The other was around five six, short blonde hair and quite stocky, Steve Roberts was his name or 'Robo' to the people who knew him. He lived in Coalpool just outside of Walsall close to where my dad was born and ran 'Spartan' martial arts classes. Rumor had it that he once gave someone an uppercut on the front door and took him out of his shoes!

Then in came Nick the DJ.

This guy was a complete fucking nutcase .The first time I'd ever spoken to him he was shoving his dick in one of the punters mouths behind the DJ console and started swinging around doing an impression of a helicopter. A few more people came in over the next few minuets. First was Hagga who was 10feet wide and hard as nails. I once saw him knock a man out with a 6 inch punch. Tony Brookes, Pigeon, Chrissie Phipps followed and Tony Dutton who owned Tony's Gym in Brownhills. Unfortunately he passed away some years ago, may God bless him, I could think of a lot more people who deserved to go than Tony, but Life's a funny old game eh?

Then Sharon, Graham's girlfriend appeared. She helped me out of a few situations as the years went on with references for the 'Old Bill' saying I was a good boy and trustworthy, you know the one. "Cheers Shaz"

She was the one who did all the running about, controlling the staff wages, accounts etc, and putting the people in their places. What I'm trying to tell you is that no one fucked around with Sharon O'Grady, get me?

Around another eight or ten people came in, bar staff, glass collectors, cleaners and a few more doormen.

Ok, everyone got into position, making sure that all the tills were full of change, spirits topped up and straws on the bar. We were just about to open when the back door swung open and in walked my old friend Glen Noad.

"Fuck me," I said," I didn't know you worked here."

We used to get up to some right proper naughties years ago. He was the farther of my Cousin Sue's children Becky and Paul.

I liked it here and knew the party had only just begun.

The front doors were unlocked and in bowled the customers. First to come in were a bunch of five girls all wearing black hot pants and bra tops. The one at the front was proper fit looking and her pants were pulled up so tight she looked like she'd been hit between the legs with an axe if you know what I mean? They all strolled up to the bar swinging their sexy little hips the way chicks do and asked for five 'Sex on the beach.'

I looked at Glen and he laughed back knowing that they wanted a cocktail, but I thought that I was getting a six some and replied "Sorry love we're in fucking Walsall, the best thing I can offer you is the pile of builder's sand out the back if you fancy shagging on that, but it's pissing down outside so will the toilets do?

All the girls screamed with laughter and told me they'd be coming back for second helpings later. I liked it here, Pussy Galore!

Bar work was a good morale booster. It made you feel proper confident and as the night went on more and more pissed girls were coming to the bar asking my name and passing phone numbers to me for sessions after work.

The bar started to get a little quieter as the night went on and Sharon asked me if I could collect a few of the glasses as we were running short. I grabbed a tray and started to wonder around.

This night we were doing a 'Grolsh' promotion and there were bottles all over the floor. Just as I was about to crouch down to pick a few up from the floor I noticed that the five girls from earlier had surrounded me.

Now, glass collectors from all over the world will understand when I tell you if you've got a tray full of bottles and a few others in your hands, you always get the dolly's poking and prodding you in places and feeling your arse, because they know you cant do fuck all about it!

Well, this lot spotted me and when I crouched down two of them grabbed my bollocks while one of the others pulled up her skirt to reveal a nice set of sexy black stocking and suspenders. Now don't you love it when that happens eh?

The dirty fucker just stood there and her mates closed around us so that no one could see what was going on!

Just for the record a friend of mine who I won't mention his name for marital reasons did the same some weeks later , but came up looking like he'd been smacked in the gob with a tomato ketchup bottle!

Some girls make me laugh. I mean, a bloke lobs his tool out in a bar and he's a dirty bastard and here I had a circle of them watching the re make of *'Lassie come home'* and none of them gave a fuck. Mad innit?

So, anyway I had my supper and started to circle the building for more glasses. I walked over to the corner of one of the bars, where there was a crowd of rowdy lads playing up big time with three tidy looking Sutton girls. These were the Broadhursts, John, Christian, Butch, Danny and a few of the O Grady's, Roy, Andrew, Booey and friend Spen.

Now I must tell you that if you put this lot together in one place, play up is not the word. They'd stand up the bar all night supping bottles of Don Perigion champagne and Buds until they came out of their ears and then decide to give out as much 'stick' as they possibly could to every fucker.

Graham used to go mental, but at the end of the day they did spunk some dosh so he kind of stood for it you know.

I think JB had the record for the most spit roasts with Booey not far behind him.

Oh, and not forgetting the Perv, he used to spot a fight and try to find little gaps in the crowd to creep up and whack 'em on the jaw to knock 'em out.

I remember when we were at the steelworks in Bilport Lane in Wendsbury and the Perv had whacked someone who hadn't gone down. He ran from the bottom to the top of the road, which is about half a mile long to where we were sitting in Milky's unit. He tried to hide in the Porta cabin, but we wouldn't open the door to let him in. Eventually we let him in and shortly after the bloke turned up banging on the cabin doors going mad, the Perv hid behind Milkys desk begging for us not to open the door!

As the weeks went on Graham decided to give the Broadhursts their own bar at the top of the club to stop them abusing the rest of the punters, and me, being the only one who really got on with them, was nominated to be their personal Tom Cruise.

I used to some nights walk out of there with a few hundred quid in tips and an odd behind the bar blow job from one of the girls for being ever such a good fuckin' host.

Good times were had at The Dilke fun pub, where all the staff had used to get on really well, Tracey, Glen, Sharon, Stevie, Mel, Teresa, Damian, and DJ Paul Jones who I can honestly say was one of the blaggers of all time!

Then, there was my good friend Big Jim, Derek the dancing doorman, Gary Baker , Loza, Jase, 'Go Go' Fernando the Gay Indian Dj, who looked like Sanjay from East enders and last but by no means least Darren and Craig Pinches who were Grahams brothers and I must add were my partners in Party for some years on the Walsall scene.

It was ten minutes to one and in 1990 the clubs only had a license until one in the morning as the laws were somewhat stricter than today, so the bar started to close and I'd gone back on a mission to collect glasses, bottles, and as many telephone numbers as I could.

The toilets were full of sick and over flowing, where the dick heads had wedged toilet rolls in the u bends or 'hughey' bends as we used to call them.

Still, I could never work out the 'Carrot mystery'. Even if you'd not eaten a thing for two days the fucking things would pop up, and when the toilets were full of puke with shit floating spilling over the sides, you'd always get some cunt still pissing on top of it all and flooding the toilet floors.

The next day the sides would drop out of your shoes and there'd be no bottoms left in your fuckin socks, filthy bastards , got no respect. You'd be better off trying to have one in the ladies, at least then you may have a chance of grabbin a bit of squashed hedgehog lads ,ya get me?

The majority of the time the ladies would be worse than the men's though, with broken glass everywhere.

Once I went in to check the women's for damages and someone had written their name across the mirror with one of those disposable red and white candles!

Tasty, the birds are in Walsall aren't they eh? Never been into blood sports myself, but I dare say she may have won a prize on take art, who knows?

Craig had a club in Maidstone called Harriet's. Graham and I had visited him once on a trip to Paris, via Dover, to get some ideas for the new bar refurbishment.

It was quite late when we got there and I remember we had our heads down on the sofa in Craig's front room of the flat above the club.

At around 3am in the morning I woke up bursting for a piss but couldn't find the light switch, so I opened the living room door and tried to find my way to the toilet. I got half way across the landing, slid on the floor, went arse over tit and then got attacked by Craig's giant Alsatian, Ben.

Craig came out of his bedroom and switched on the light screaming with laughter as he called the dog off me.

What the cunt hadn't told me was that at night this is where his trusty guard dog used to sleep and not only that, but the landing was covered completely in sloppy dog shit. So there I was lying there with a five stone Alsatian mauling me, covered from head to toe in recycled Chappie! Graham nearly pissed himself laughing as I'd only brought two changes of clothes.

I spent the next two days walking around Paris smelling like some cunt from Dynarod.

When Craig decided that London was no longer for him he came up to play in Walsall. In the early nineties there was a seedy Blues club in town called 'The City Slicker' in Bradford Street that was up for grabs and he'd decided to re open it as an American theme bar.

I think it cost three hundred quid to do the total refurbishment and had been completed in less than ten hours.

How the fuck can you refurbish a two story venue in less than ten hours you're probably thinking, right?

First of all forget hiring painters and decorators they're time consuming and expensive. You just go to every video rental shop in the town and ask them to give you as many posters as they can advertising new and old films they had in stock.

We stapled the fuckers all over the walls, holes in the ceilings, smashed glass windows, every where you could imagine.

When we eventually finished it looked like a giant version of Blockbusters. Pop over the road to Latif's and grab 200ft of bunting flags and hey presto eat your heart out T.G.I Fridays!

Walsall people aren't really that hard to please either. We'd bought an old fashioned Ambulance, in fact old wasn't the word. I think it was pre 'Dixon of Dock Green,' one of those wide, big, high topped ones. We fixed it up and did a bit of welding on it, because it was basically dropping to bits. We then used it to supply all the punters a transfer from the Dilke to the newly opened 'Bradford Place American theme bar' which was about two miles down the road.

The majority of the girls used to complain and say that they didn't want to wear the crash helmets we'd supplied for the journey as it messed up their hair do's. A free trip to another venue in those days was unheard of, but I'm sure a few of them knew the chauffer had been banned from driving for five years and had sunk enough Jack Daniels to be five times over the limit. Not only that, Geoff the chef 'God bless him' had told us that the MOT he'd got us was *cosha*, but when you held it up to the light you could see where it hadn't been soaked in the brake fluid long enough and read 'Ford Cortina 1300e 4 door!'

We all missed Geoff as he passed away a few years later. Whenever you'd see him he'd be completely leathered and he would always say

"I've only had two", in proper slurred voice, even though you'd just bought him four.

I worked with him in the kitchens at various venues and can tell you he was a top bloke.

"Rest in Peace mate."

Bradford place opened with a bang. It took half the pissed punters from the Dilke and the rest came from the local town pubs after hours. It was amazing that we never got nicked by the old bill because, after two or three journeys back and forth in the old ambulance down the Melish road we started to leave a trail like someone had stuck two giant smoke machines to the back of it. I calculated that it must have only done about twelve miles to the gallon, but that was fuckin' oil I was talking about not petro! It also had a sign in the front window saying 'Tax in post'. You could half get away with it in those days and the good thing was that if the old bill had been behind us, they wouldn't have been able to see because of the amount of smoke, whether it was a car or a fucking' airplane that they were chasing, never mind be able to see the registration plate!

'Oh the good old days.'

BANGED UP ABROAD

Just a minute, you'll have to excuse me.

Oh, I didn't tell you that I'm writing this book from my prison cell in a Tenerife penitentiary in the Canary Islands.

A few so called friends and I got banged up for currency forgery and fraud a few months ago on the 16th of august 2003.

The cunt who's just been padded up with me in cell number 51 had told me a load of old bollocks about why he'd ended up here and someone in 'the know' has just informed us that he'd raped a woman down in the south of the island and is now trying to keep it 'hush hush.'

He's a huge French African man, who snores like a fuckin' diesel engine and while he was out last night I filled his tube of pile cream with tooth paste and his tooth paste with pile cream.

He's not sleeping tonight trust me, his ass will be on fire and his mouth should have healed up by the morning, the cunt him.

Bradford Place was full to the brim and the town had never seen so many people crammed into one building on a Thursday night.

The punters who had come from the Dilke were fine in the looks and the dress department, but the townies were a bit worse for wear.

If you had never been on a night out in Walsall in the nineties there wasn't many places open in the town centre after eleven o clock, so you'd get all sorts of life loitering around looking for watering holes to finish off in.

DJ Nick and I had just dropped off the last load to the club and headed off to Bradford Place in a 3 litre S Capri which I'd bought the week before.

There were five of us in the car and on the way up the Melish road we'd spotted eight girls who were walking up the street because they'd missed the last bus home. We pulled over and asked them if they'd fancy a lift to our new club in the town.

We somehow managed to fit thirteen people in the car, and as we drove away you could see lots of sparks flying out of the back where the exhaust pipes were dragging on the floor. The car looked like a giant fuckin' firework with arms and legs sticking out all of the windows.

Two of the girls, who I'd put in the boot wore nice white dresses and when we'd eventually reached the Homebase car park ,had all untangled arms and legs to get out, I lifted the hatch forgetting that I'd put a load of old car engine parts in the back.

The two girls jumped out looking like a couple of 'Kwik fit fitters' and were covered from head to toe in oil and axle grease. It was matted in their hair and they'd got piston rings for earrings.

They were not amused at all. I gave them free entry tickets and they sat down in a dark corner of the club out of sight.

If my memory serves me right I think I shagged one of them that same night, but she stank that much I fucked her off out my bed. Just no turn on for me that 'Diesel for women.'

TENERIFE II

The Belgian rapist has just been carted off to the prison hospital with breathing problems.

He did brush his teeth last night and kept looking at me real funny, as if he'd suspected something.

This morning he must have 'wapped' that pile cream on his arse, because his eyes have been watering since the early hours.

Knowing my luck I'll get a visit off the Governor today with an extra charge of attempted 'ass'assination!

Twelve months later, Graham and Craig had turned the Bradford Place into a nice little earner.

It was 'chocker' Wed, Thurs, Fri and Saturday.

Now I know it wasn't the classiest of places but Gray being Gray used to charge prices higher than 'String fellows' in London.

The once I could remember talking to a bloke at about 1:30am in the morning pissed out of my brains on Diamond whites. I don't think he could understand a fucking word I was saying. The thing was when you were drinking those you acquired a language of your own. Now if you're pissed on something else and you try to chat to someone who'd been drinking Diamond whites you could no way communicate with them, It's like speaking Portuguese to a Hungarian if you like, it just won't happen, but, if you were both drinking Diamond whites you could talk all night without problem, strange shit that?

As for shows, I've done more in Walsall than Robbie Williams has done in his whole fucking' career after closing times!

'Bushwackers,' which had not long been opened by Darren, Craig and Graham, was an Australian themed wine bar and was situated some 20 meters from Bradford Place.

One Wednesday night Danny and I were just starting to close up after a 'Ladies drink free night' which as you could expect had a certain sparkle to it.

Around 11:30 I'd spotted a very good looking but reserved girl drinking at the bar. She was alone and had long blonde hair just like the girl off the 'Timote shampoo' advert who used to wash her long locks in the lake, or in this case canal, as we were in Walsall!

Anyway, just before we locked the door I strolled over and asked her if she'd like to stay for a drink after time.

She was dressed in jeans, a white long wool cardigan and seemed somewhat under dressed for her age, with a pretty shy looking face.

The bar closed up and most of the staff left So we grabbed a few drinks and the three of us sat down in the dim lit corner of the bay seating area and introduced ourselves.

She told us her name was Wendy and lived locally. We sat there for a while and completely out of the blue she said

"Shall we play spin the bottle?"

I looked at Johnny and he looked at me. We both burst out laughing as between us we'd span more bottles than Tom Cruise.

"Oh, go on then," we both said in sync, as if it'd been all pre rehearsed, and we let the games begin.

We wiped the table, placed an empty bottle of Budweiser on top then Wendy nominated herself to spin first. Just my fucking luck it landed on me.

"Ok," she said pointing her finger at me, "Fucking strip."

"Sorry?" I replied

"You heard me, strip," she repeated.

Have you ever been to one of those church jumble sales when the doors have just been opened and there's fifty women throwing clothes over their shoulders looking for a bargain before anyone else gets there?

So there I sat bottle in one hand and dick in the other at the table hoping the fuck I don't see the tip of the fucker pointing in my direction on this spin. Remembering the rules 'You can't spin on yourself' made me feel a little better. Now it was my turn. The bottle span fast as we all stared for a few seconds to see who would be the next victim.

This time around it pointed to Danny, and because he'd found it quite hilarious what had just happened to me I thought I'd return the favour.

"You choose Wendy," I said with a smirk on my face.

"You can't do that yer cunt," he screamed, "The spinner has to nominate."

"Ok then, I shall nominate her to nominate," I replied.

"Strip bollock naked," she told him.

I spat out half my drink as he gave me one of those 'you cunt looks' and stripped his kit off.

So there we were, and you're probably thinking that this girl had us right at it, and any moment now she was going to make a sharp exit, right?

The bottle span again, and this time it landed on her. Both in harmony we said it was her turn to do the same, giggling like two little kids whilst doing so.

She stood up away from the table, and for a split second we did actually think she was off. Underneath her dull white cardigan and tatty jeans, (which she took off quicker than Dj Fernando can fuck a fat bloke, and believe me, that's fucking quick!) She had a Basque, black stockings and suspenders, the whole kit on!

"Fuck me, Bargain!" I screamed, as we sat there with our chins dragging on the floor because we thought that this porn star was a librarian. Realizing we'd hit the jackpot we both started to buzz.

The bottle spun around a few times more and before we knew it she was on all fours blowing me off. Danny then went to the condom machine in the toilets and came back with a funny look on his face, as all he could manage to get was one of those 'fun condoms' from the machine on the wall. There was nothing fun about them because if you've ever used one you'll know they're harder to put on than a wet marigold glove!

I could see him fumbling around at the back of her arse, which was in the air and patiently waiting for the 'back shot', I could see that his head was shaking from side to side because he couldn't put it on.

I'm sure at one point he was wearing her stockings and suspenders as well! (Just joking)

What he hadn't told me until later was that while she was playing the flute he could smell something that resembled cheese on toast? But couldn't work out where the smell was coming from.

"Then my dick couldn't make its mind up weather it was going north or south." He went on to tell me.

Thing was, it was the middle of summer at the time and everyone was wearing leather shoe sandals. I was working seven days a week and most nights too and my poor old shoes had suffered a hammering. I'd taken them off and kicked them over the other side of the table which by chance was where he had been kneeling, so that every time he'd bent down towards her ass he could smell them. He thought that it was her that stunk and I ended up having to finish the job off myself!

After hearing about our escapades everyone started sniffing around her, in fact Bushwackers over the road had started to get quite full on a Wednesday and Thursday night.

DJ Fernando fancied his chances the one night and we'd arranged for him to have a secret rendezvous in the flat above the bar. Before I sent Wendy upstairs I whispered a little something into her ear.

We waited fifteen minutes and all went up to see what was happening.

We all walked in as she was giving him *'The motorbike'* you know the one where the girl wanks you off like she's twisting back on the accelerator of a motorbike, but dead fast. You don't? You ain't lived.

He'd kneeled on the bed with a big smile and then all of a sudden his face changed to that of a china man having a shit after a hot curry.

What I hadn't told him was that I'd informed her that my dear friend Fernando liked to be covered in baby oil and have a bird shove her fingers up his arse. So, while she was blowing him I'd passed her a bottle of hair conditioner and she covered her hands in it and shoved her 4 fingers up his arse!

His face changed a third time which worried me a little because a smile appeared again.

I never looked at him the same since that night if you get my drift.

I was sure in the back of my mind he didn't know whether he was batting or bowling anymore?

"Oh the night is my world.

City lights- painted gold.

In the day nothing flatters.

It's the night-time that matters."

DRUGS MUGS AND THUGS

"What's your name?"
"What you had?"
"Where do you come from?"

Have to be the three most famous questions that are asked on the club scene, more than any others in the whole world.

Even if you couldn't talk because you were coming up on a triple drop, your eyesight was fucked and your mind was in a mess, you could always manage to give out the compulsory nod and blow out of air with lips pouted just to let the other person know that you were having a proper fucking ball!

Then, you feel the rush of the second pill kick in , your breathing gets deeper and deeper until you're speechless ,your eyes start to flicker or even close for a few seconds. Your body is now rushing from head to toe. Jaw lock sets in, your teeth start to grind and everything around you becomes a blur. You can feel the bass drumming into your chest which amplifies everything. You then start to level out, but a second later another rush hits you and this time your head feels like a fucking volcano waiting to erupt. Now you're wishing you never took that third pill and hope it doesn't get any worse, but it does. You start tripping. The People all around you are dancing, everything turns into slow motion, and then your body becomes paralysed and starts to rock from side to side which makes your balance go 'A wire.' You look left and see someone crouching with his back to the wall with the same look on his face. You know this is where you want to be, but even though your mind tells you to go your legs are having none of it. Someone passes you a J.D .and coke. You gulp it down hoping that it may take the edge of the mind blowing rushes you're experiencing, but no, there's plenty more where that came from, and you thought that you were pretty fucking brave when everyone saw you pop those three little fellows, didn't you?

Now I didn't start popping pills and sticking devils dandruff up my nose until early '95'. Two new clubs had opened up in Bentley near Walsall called Ethos and the Zone. They weren't like the proper underground clubs in the city, but more commercial type venues .They both had 4000 capacity each and were joined together by a small hallway with double doors at both ends. The door policy was that of similar commercial clubs in town .No trainers, shirts at weekends and trousers or dark jeans if you were a regular.

Hort was six feet three, medium build with light brown blondish hair and in the 'nineties' we were rarely apart as we were both as mad as hatters, and no one could keep up with us!

It was a Thursday night. Not that it made any difference as Hort and I were out every single night getting terribly shitfaced and giving out as much abuse as humanly possible.

We got inside at around 10:30ish .The Zone had just started a new dance night and had shipped a few DJ's in from Birmingham's club scene. The place was full of dollies, some of them tidy and others looking like 'Hilda Ogden' on smack, but that's Walsall, you just had to live with it!

Hort and I walked up to the bar, shuffled to the front and ordered two large JD and cokes.

There was something about tonight I just couldn't get a grip on. It seemed different somehow. The people all wore smiles, not normal ones, but like they'd all won the lottery.

"Fuck me Hort it's buzzing in here, look at that gang of birds over there," I said pointing.

He looked over and a group of five girls were staring in our direction wearing big luring smiles. Three of them were fit and the other two looked like a pair of car mechanics, but never the less they were happy about something.

I looked down to see if my dick was hanging out, but it wasn't. Mr. wriggly was in his sleeping bag fast asleep for the minute, maybe he'd make an appearance later, who knows?

We walked over, "Alright ladies?" This was Hort's all time ice breaker, and then he'd usually follow up with 'fancy a sausage cob?'

The girls giggled.

Hort had this strange way of pulling the birds. He used to do this mad dance that resembled the mating ceremony of a peacock on acid, but for some unknown reason he got results. I sometimes wondered whether he hypnotized them with his arm and leg movements.

Anyway, off he went, first spinning around three times as fast as he could, forgetting that he still had a full drink in his hand and drowning everyone within ten meters of his fit. He then switched to the Hawaiian 'Rah Rah' dance where you make both hands do a wave motion. Two waves to the left and two to the right, Then 'Saturday night fever', 'Staying alive', 'The birdie song', 'The moonwalk', 'Body popping', 'Break dancing', 'Wigfields Saturday night dance', The twist', 'Russian vodka dance', 'Kung fu', 'Kickboxing', then 'Hopping on one leg whilst doing an impression of a windmill' .He was getting faster and faster until you could just see a blur. He eventually tripped himself up as he was going so fast a fell flat on his arse. All five girls just stood there eyes fixed and mouths wide open as if they' just witnessed the appearance of an extra terrestrial.

"Come on ladies," he sang, jumping into the press up position. He attempted to spin on his head, but could only manage to lift his legs off the floor for a split second. When he'd realized it wasn't happening he just ran around in circles with his head still on the carpet and both arms waving in the air.

Security came over. By this time there must have been fifty people around us clapping at the exhibition .Hort was definitely without a doubt a crowd puller!

I reached out my hand to help him up just as one of the doormen broke into the empty circle which Hort had just had an epileptic fit in.

"What the fucks going on here?" he growled.

The doorman was around 5 feet 8inches tall and by the acne and boyish looks on his face I reckoned he was about 20 years old, with the attitude of 'Arnies bigger brother'. His chest was full of air with 'I'm a tough bastard' written across his face.

"He just tripped up on a bottle someone had thrown on the floor mate, that's all," I said, trying not to laugh.

"The dance floors over there" replied the doorman, "What pills has he been on?" he added, smiling and walking away.

Then it clicked!

"Come on Hort, let's go for a walk," I said

The more and more people I looked at I realized that 90% of the club were on drugs, absolutely off their tits, all of them chewing gum, jaws going 100 mph with eyes wide like dinner plates and they were bouncing to the rocking beats being played by the DJ.

I looked to my left and Hort had disappeared. I scanned around the club to see if I could see his head bobbing about. Being so tall he wasn't normally the hardest person to find in a crowd, but he was nowhere to be seen this time. I walked back over to the bar and paid for a couple more drinks.

The Zone had two levels with steep flights of stairs at either side, two large bars downstairs and six podiums around the edges of the dance floor, which were at this time occupied by dancers dressed in skimpy bikinis with knee high fluffy boots. All of them wore hairstyles like they'd been plugged into the electricity mains and it was dyed bright red. Their bodies were covered from head to toe in silver glitter and looking up I noticed they had bright coloured glow sticks which made trails as they were swooped through the dark smoke filled air.

"Fuck me Shane where've you been?" said Hort on his return "I've been looking everywhere for you."

"Well I've been looking for you too Hort."

"I just went for a piss next door and when I got back you'd disappeared," he replied, as if it was my fault for not being telepathic.

"Robert, have a good look at everyone in here, they're all 'off it'," I said, eager to share my discovery. "Shall we get some E's?"

There was a pause and I pictured the reels going round on one of those big square computers from the old films, red and yellow lights and all. He quickly made his analysis "I will if you will?" Hort replied.

"They can't be that bad if everyone's on 'em, can they?" I said, trying to play it down that we were now starting to take drugs.

We walked around the edges of the dance floor hoping we could find someone selling something, anything! An hour later, still nothing.

"Let's try the dance floor," I shouted, "Look for the fucker with the biggest eyes and ask him what he's had."

It sounded like the best plan of action. The person with the biggest eyes must have the best gear right?

We shuffled through the heaving crowds looking at everyone's expressions individually for the tell tale signs of what we were about to look like.

There was a small gap in the crowd on the dance floor about ten people in front of us where a group of four were dancing, consisting of three girls and one lad in his late teens. As we got closer I could see that his eyes were pinned back like he'd just seen a ghost, his jaw was locked and slanted to the side and he resembled a cow chewing grass. 'This was our boy!'

I walked to the side of him and tapped him on his shoulder. He looked up at me, smiled and nodded his head as if I'd just asked him if he wanted five hundred quid for free. His cheesy grin and saucer like eyes told me he was definitely not on 'this' planet!

"Got any pills mate?" I shouted, trying to overcome the huge base pumping out of the twelve feet high speakers that were in the four corners of the dance floor. He nodded again.

This bloke hadn't got a fuckin' clue what I was talking about , in fact, if I had of said 'Your old lady's on the game and you dad takes it up the chocker dubie' he would of done exactly the same, bless him.

I grabbed his arm and pulled him into a quieter section close to the edge of the podiums. One of the dancers was climbing down with her bikini bottoms pulled up the crack of her arse because of all the dancing she'd been doing, her body was dripping with sweat like she'd just got out of the shower.

"Hi cheeky." I said, as she looked down at me and smiled, gulping down half a bottle of water as if her life depended on it.

I put my head close to the lad's ear. "Listen mate, I want to buy some pills. Have you got any?"

"Yeah geez', proper Doves, 'tens' each," he said.

"Give me two." I told him.

He slid his hand into the small pocket on the front right hand side of his jeans and pulled out a transparent zippy bag. Inside I could see he had around eight pills left.

"Give me four," I told him, as I'd calculated that if it took us this long to find someone who'd got gear sober, we'd got no chance of getting any more after popping two of those baby's. In fact, by the look of his friend who'd just joined us, I was wondering whether I'd still remember my fucking name after the first one. I gave him two twenty's.

"These are dancers mate, proper dancers!"

I nodded trying not to look concerned with the weird pill faces he kept on pulling. He wouldn't have looked out of place in the cast of 'One flew over the cuckoo's nest' for sure.

"Nice one mate, have a good one," he said, touching my arm as he and his freaky friend bounced off to the spot I'd found him at earlier.

Right, that was it. We got our kit and walked off to the toilets over the far side of the club and decided the best place to see what we'd scored was in the cubicles.

The tablets were flat, off white grayish colour with a split in the back. There was a pair of doves imprinted in the centre and they had a slight shine to them. I felt butterflies hovering round in my stomach.

"There you go Hort, two for you and two for me," I said, passing him his half share.

We both looked at each other as if to say 'should we really be doing this,' but in the back of our minds we knew that the job had to be done.

I put the pill on my tongue and took a gulp of the JD to send it down the hatch. No matter how I tried there must have been a dry patch somewhere in my mouth or throat because I just couldn't swallow it properly. The pill ended up back on my tongue already breaking up from the liquid I'd added to it, and then seconds later the most putrid taste in the world. It was like I'd been sucking on Gandhi's flip flop. I took another big gulp and away she went. Now there was no turning back.

"Go on then Robert, get it down ya then," I said.

"I'll have mine in a minute," he replied.

Not daft is he Hort? I think he was waiting to see if I died first, then he wouldn't have taken his.

Eventually he did, rocking his head back a few times as he tried his best to get it down without having the same trouble I'd had a few minuets earlier.

"That's it now Shane, do or die!"

"Nice one Hort," I said, "that was the last thing I needed to hear after popping my first E."

All of a sudden I felt sick and my face looked as if all the blood had been drained from it. My stomach started to churn and I broke out into a sweat. There was no air conditioning in the toilets and the high powered spot lights which were inset into the ceiling gave off an intense heat as they shined onto my head. I made a dash for the cubicle but it was locked. I felt my stomach contract and the Mc Donald's I'd eaten for dinner with strawberry milkshake vaulted upwards toward my throat. I banged on the cubicle door to try and get whoever was dumping in there to get the fuck out, but no doors opened. My mouth filled with sick, but still the doors didn't open. I couldn't waste the pill id just popped, so I just swallowed the warm puke back down and swigged the remainder of my drink to get rid of the acidic taste left in my mouth. My hand banged down hard on the tap and the water gushed into the sink spraying up my shirt as I cupped my hands together trying to catch enough to drench my burning face.

"Fucking hell Shane, you alright?"

Hort looked worried and this didn't help. After a few minutes I felt calmer. I took a few deep breathes and started to get my head back together.

Hort rubbed the middle of his chest around in circles. "Ooh, this was a bad move Shane," he said, shaking his head from side to side thinking he'd got the same to come.

"Nah, we'll be ok, I think it was the food I ate earlier. Come on lets get the fuck out of here, it's too hot," I said, trying to play the situation down.

We pushed through the two spring loaded doors back into the deafening club and walked to the bar which was on our right hand side as we left the toilets. I felt quite normal again after sinking half a glass of someone else's

Vodka, but I knew that the normality was only going to last another thirty minutes or so.

"Let's go and have a nose about," said Hort, walking off scanning the nearby talent which had just entered from 'Ethos' next door. We walked round the chromed rails which separated the raised floor around the bar area and headed towards the gap that led to the dance floor opposite the main entrance.

By this time the building was absolutely rammed, the dance floor was heaving and they announced that Boy George had taken over the decks, which made the crowds cheer and scream as the first tune kicked in.

I felt a warm feeling in my lower chest and my head started to tingle slightly. The bass vibrated throughout my body which in turn started my head nodding to the beat of the drums. I looked to my right and Hort had started chewing his Wrigley at hyper speed.

"Are you getting a tickle of that yet Robert?" I asked.

"Fuck knows Shane, something's going on though," he replied, looking a little edgy.

I could see his eyes starting to widen and his chest filling with air. He took a swig of his Budweiser and emptied his lungs as if he was trying to cool down a cup of hot tea. I yawned and as I did so felt a rush from the top to the bottom of my spine. It felt as if someone was trying to possess me and trust me they weren't doing a bad job either!

"Buckle up your seat belt Dorothy we're on our way to the Land of Oz," I said, laughing as my jaw started to lock up and another rush it me from head to toe. Within a few minutes we had both started hyperventilating and were leaning on the side of the podiums.

"Fucking hell, this is kicking the shit out of me."

"And me," replied Hort, panting like he'd just crossed the finish line after beating Lynford Christie at the hundred meters.

We both stood there for a good fifteen minutes rushing our bollocks off, and after leveling out for a little while I decided to go to the toilets.

I walked back passed the rails surrounding the bar and started to head towards the entrance. As I slid through the crowds I noticed that everyone was looking at me, especially the girls. The music sounded 'propa' and I broke out into a dance thrusting my hands into the air as I passed everyone with my lips pouted and head nodding backwards and forwards to the beat of the pumping bass.

I got to the toilets with my head still nodding and waited for the next space to piss became available. Turning around and looking in the mirror it dawned on me that I had indeed been possessed .My eyes were virtually popping out of my head and my lips looked like Mick Jagger's singing 'I can't get no satisfaction.' I looked the dog's bollocks, no wonder all the girls were staring at me. I waited for everyone to leave the toilets and did a little dance in the mirror to see how 'propa' I looked. I was sure I looked better than anyone else in the club and after the ego injection of seeing myself looking so good, I was convinced that I was the main man.

I took a piss and had a last glance in the mirror grinning to myself as I opened the door to partyville.

The tunes were blurring. 'Sugar daddy set me free…'

I scanned the bar area with the smile of a Cheshire cat. I noticed that at the end of the bar a few people were pointing in the direction of where I'd left Hort earlier.

I looked up.

While I'd been in the toilets he'd climbed the metal ladder up to the podium, jumped on to the platform and started to spin one of the dancers around in circles, shirt half hanging out and pissing of sweat.

The pill had definitely done its job!

I knew exactly how he felt. I now felt super human, I was buzzing like a nuclear reactor and the music felt like it was in perfect sync with my brain waves. As I stood next to one of the huge bass bins on the edge of the dance floor I nearly passed out because the bass amplified the buzz tenfold. It was a better feeling than getting a tit wank off Pamela Anderson and I was sure if she'd of been there I could of pulled her easy as well!

Security came over and told Hort he needed to be getting down from the podium. The dancer looked distressed, but Hort just carried on dancing and gave him the finger. Two more doormen came over and I tugged at his trouser leg telling him we were going to get chucked out if he didn't come down.

Eventually, he did and we headed for the dance floor. They could have been playing the Queens national anthem for all we cared it wouldn't have stopped us dancing; anything loud with a beat as far as we were concerned sounded the bollocks.

One thing I'd definitely noticed about those Doves was that, not only did they make you feel unbelievably confident and happy, but they made the girls all look like darlings. This could be kind of dangerous if you think about it because you could be giving it your best shot and largin it with the lads about the 'mint' little lady you'd just pulled, then when the pills started to wear off at the end of the night your prize catch could of turned into your next door neighbours window cleaner. Trust me, that's not good for the ego when everyone else had seen it a few hours before but hadn't got the heart to tell you because you were too 'off your cake', Some mates!

I looked at my watch, it read 01:33am I think my eyes were struggling to focus with all of the smoke and lasers that were flying through the air. We had just half an hour left before last orders. I realized something else about the magic pills, they also made you extra generous because I found myself buying half the people at the bar a drink, at this rate I'd be bankrupt by a quarter to and I didn't even know any of them!

Hort had a theory about women, and that was if you chatted to every single girl in the club at the end of the night you must definitely get the ride off one of them.

As I looked to my left I saw he'd got two new recruits who were being spun around at lightning speed.

My dad always used to tell me 'Once you get 'em laughing son your half way in their knickers' and how right he was. His best mate Johnny Hickinbottom once said that when he was my age my dad would have shagged a frog if he could have stopped it jumping, which is probably where I got it from. Like father like son and all.

The lights came on and the music volume dropped. The two blonde birds looked a bit tatty around the edges, but by no means ugly, anyway Hort and I must have looked like a pair of Kentucky fried nutcases with our jaws going a 100 miles per hour, side to side and eyes like ping pong balls. We couldn't keep still for any amount of time.

A taxi arrived outside for us and we all jumped in the back. The smaller blonde of the two had what my mate Nick the Dj called an 'Airplane skirt' on because it was so short that it was only two inches from the 'cock pit.' Terrible I know but you'd had to of met him to appreciate him.

This little lady was mine. She snuggled up to me on the back seat of the cab trying to make out she was really cold, but there was no sign of goose bumps on her legs and not only that, she was a crap actress , you know the one,

"Ooooooh its freezing"

I played along anyway (it would be rude not to wouldn't it?) and covered us both with my coat. The inside of my mouth felt like I'd been chewing glass and my tongue was sore as fuck through biting it for the last few hours on the 'pillathon'

Now the little dolly who pretended to be cold earlier started to move her hand down from my chest trying to let each movement go unnoticed by shuffling her body from side to side as if she was uncomfortable.

Before I knew it, my flies were down and the five knuckle shuffle was in full swing, all that and the cheeky sod hadn't even asked me my name. Her head went under the coat and was bobbing up and down.

"Fuck me Hort, this one could suck a basket ball through a straw," I said.

"G'on Shane give it some," Hort shouted, eyes wide looking for a piece of action.

The other girl next to Hort must have got all turned on by seeing her mate play the flute, and pulled up her red sequined micro skirt and started to play with her giggling pin (if you don't know what that is you want to be getting a life!) She reached out and pulled my hand towards her now wide open legs which made her look like she was waiting for a train.

I put my hand on the back of the girl's head that was still blowing me off at the speed of light and told her to swap to Hort. Before I'd finished my sentence she'd done a 180 degree turn and started to work .I moved forward and started to bang her mate who, may I add, was a wet as as window cleaner's leather at this point.

The taxi driver pulled up and told us as we'd reached our destination. When he realised what had been going on he started to giggle and said with one of those broad Black Country, Asian accents, "Bloody hell matey; could you not of being waiting until you are getting home?"

I reached down by my knees and pulled the last two tenners from my creased trouser pockets and handed him one.

"Drive around the block our kid and I'll give you another fiver," I said with my arse still swinging ten to the dozen.

"Ok boss," he replied, winking and smiling as he pulled off.

By this time Hort was getting his oats. Shortly after he started pulling one of those strange faces that the men pull on the porno films when they're 'booting their loot.'

"You ain't finished yet Robert, have you?" I asked.

I think it must have been the pills that gave him that look, but it was fucking funny anyway.

Taxi drivers in Walsall aren't stupid mate, believe me. By the time we'd finished our business we were another fifteen quid out of pocket because the fucking driver drove as fast as he could, which meant we'd gone around the block three times! Have you ever had a foursome in the back of a black cab with Lewis Hamilton driving? Trust me, all four of us were battered and bruised.

Shortly after Hort I and decided we were hungry and told the girls to wait in the cab while we went into the kebab shop for food .They gave us twenty quid towards it and Yep, you guessed it. We fucked off and didn't return.

Well come on, you really didn't expect us to pay for everything did you eh? Thought so!

The World Newspaper Spain   *Buckingham Palace*

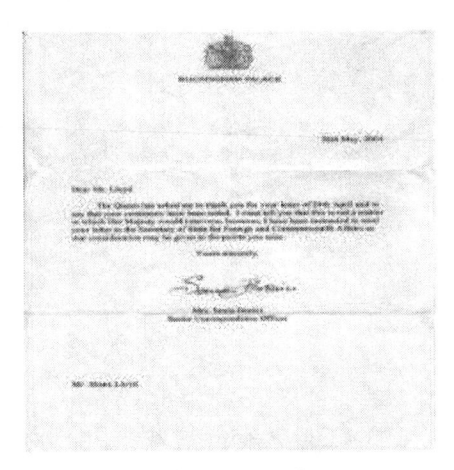

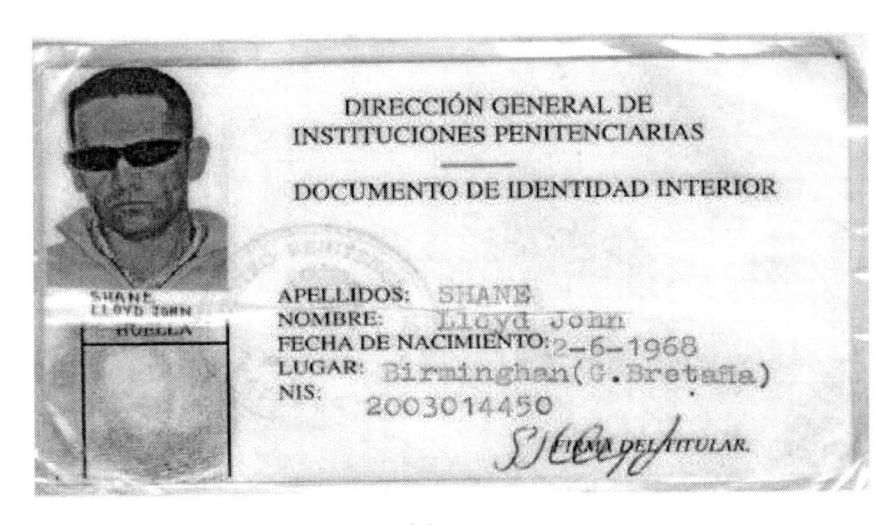

My Spanish Prison ID

Chinky Jones's Funeral

Summer @ The Monkey

Ami Harley

"This is a stick up!" Me, Paul, Sue, Donna, Bubba Cuts & John planning a Bank job in the early days.

Me Mom & Donna

'Who's the Daddy?'

Steve Pettitt, Britains Hardest Doorman.

Lotty, Stirring 'em up!

The famous Hort & Froggy Lawton.

Hermano's para siempre!

Col The Medik & Frenshy

Giles & Matt

MEET THE BOYS

Ethos and the Zone became a regular thing as they'd now started regular dance nights on a Friday and Saturday some weeks later. We ended up getting a good old crowd together each weekend.

I can remember the one Saturday night I was at the top of the stairs chatting to a Pamela Anderson look alike when I noticed standing down close to one of the rear bars were a gang of lads staring up at me, as if to say 'Who does that cunt think he is?.'

'Maybe one of them was her ex or something? Fuck knows' I thought. My mind was still fixed on the fact that I'd just snorted three crushed up pills on one of the tables upstairs with Hort, which was hitting me almost immediately. 'Sniffing stuff' enters the bloodstream straight away if you didn't know? Pamela told me that she'd catch up with me later and strutted off down the stairs with half the club glaring up at her.

Stana came over and loaded us up with two fresh bottles of DP and we walked to the bottom of the twenty feet stair case and started to walk closer to the podiums which Hort had claimed a few weeks earlier. The gang of lads I had seen earlier passed close by and were all looking 'well moody'.

"Fuck me, look at these lot Stan," I said, following their movements.

They brushed past us looking me up and down. I half gave them a smile and nodded my head to see if it was me being paranoid, but I wasn't, and they were definitely not impressed about something.

The one at the front looked sort of Italian, swaying his shoulders as he walked along. Behind him was a fair haired bloke with a tight white top on and a goatee beard, they were both oozing proper fucking attitude. The rest of them were either drug dealers or, just full out evil nutcases and gave off an aura of nothing else but trouble. I walked away and went to the toilet to build a 'Charley spliff'.

The toilets as usual were roasting hot and still gurning from the dust I'd wafted earlier, I found a cubicle and slid inside. I tipped a half gram of Columbia's finest on the cistern, remembering to first wipe it down in case any water may have been there which could have made me a very unhappy chappy! Reaching into my top pocket and pulling out a gold card, I made a line about the same length as the white part of the cigarette. I then pulled out the filter with my teeth and replaced it with a small cardboard roach; because you don't want to be filtering the Charley do you? Licking along the edge of the Marlboro light, I then rolled it over the length of the sparkling white powder and 'Hey presto' one mean fucking bugle fag! After Rolling up a tube from a flyer that I had in my back pocket, I snorted the remaining powder from the top of the cistern. I sparked it up and took a long hard toke. You could see that it was proper shit because all of the Charley bubbled, turned a nice caramel color and smelt sweet like heaven.

Within a few seconds the rush came banging on like a steam train. I closed my eyes for a few seconds and shook like someone had just thrown a bucket of frozen water over me. The cubicle door swung open and I took a look in the mirror again. 'The nutty professor' sprang to mind!

Two lads around eighteen years old walked in. I turned around, looked at them, and taking another drag of the monster Marlboro, blew the smoke in their faces.

"Alright lads? Having a good un?"

Neither one of them said a word for a few seconds .I think the psychopathic look on my face had stunned them both and they'd also took in a breath of what my lungs had just exhaled.

"For fuck sake mate, what's that you're smoking," said the taller one, as they both looked at each other with amazed half smiles.

"This, my good friends is the Devils dandruff; you want a blast, or are you, err, scared?" I replied.

Once again they looked at each other and the braver one of the two reached out his hand.

"Go on then what does it do?" he enquired.

"Just take a good hard toke and I'll let you tell me in about 'mmm' fifteen seconds," I told him.

His shoulders pushed back and he rocked from side to side like he was on a beach with sand that was burning his feet. He must have thought his mate considered him 'Charley big potatoes' for taking the plunge, but this wasn't going to be the case.

Taking the cigarette in his thumb and forefinger he put it to his lips, emptied his lungs and took an almighty drag.

I took it off him and handed it to his mate, who snatched it like a beggar would a pound coin off a passer by.

"Hold your breath for 10 seconds," I told the first one.

"And you take it easy with that fag mate or else all of the 'gear' will fall off," I told his friend, who seemed a little pissed.

At that, the greedy cunt took an almighty drag and passed it back to me.

When I glanced back at the first kid he'd just taken huge a gulp of air, his face changed colour and his breathing deepened. Both hands at this point were on the edge of the ceramic sink, his knuckles had turned white with the power of the grip.

Greedy boy blew all of his smoke out and stood silent for a few seconds waiting for his unknown buzz. Finishing the gear off I strutted through the door to the main room feeling like one of the 'X men' chuckling to myself about how mangled they'd looked on my departure.

Stana was up the VIPs bar complaining to the barman that the hundred quid bottle of DP he'd just paid for wasn't chilled enough, and explained that if he didn't get another colder one it would be stuck up his arse. Chilled it was!

I filled up two glasses and passed one to a dark headed girl with huge bazookas who was standing next to me.

"Have you got a license for those darlings?" I cheekily asked.

"I've just paid three grand for these," she replied with a smile.

The best thing to do I found in this situation is reply with

"What, they aren't fakes no way!"

"They are, feel" she'll say, and if you're really good at the end of the night you'll end up with one mean sausage roll and she'd paid for it remember, three grand or fifteen hundred a side if you share with a pal!

Stana returned from the Loo's and behind him was a crowd of people with two or three doormen amongst them.

"What's going on over there," I asked.

"The security has just chucked two kids out of the toilets. One of them was hanging over the toilets being sick and the other one had shit diarrhea all down the legs of his trousers and stunk the place out."

I spat a mouthful of champers out all over the floor as I saw Greedy boy and his companion being escorted out of the building. As they passed through the busy club you could smell the combination of warm sick and shit. Greedy boy was sooo fucked as he passed me that his arm lifted and pointed over towards me, but his mouth had stopped working. I nodded at him with one eyebrow raised and gave out a bye bye salute. 'Shouldn't have taken the piss should he?' I thought. Everyone held their mouths and noses in disgust and shortly after the 'clean team' were sent in to fumigate the toilets.

I explained what had gone on to Stana which made him nearly piss himself and the girl with the big bazookas overheard us and asked if I'd got any charley left over.

"For you sugar lips, anything. Let's go to the women's toilets it must be a mess in the men's after the shit and sick posse have been there," I told her.

So off we went into 'Ethos' next door where the toilets should have smelled more human. I took a quick look around to see if any of the security were around and slid into the women's, which to my surprise were not in the best of states themselves. Bazookas beckoned me into the second cubicle as I passed Pamela the girl I'd been chatting to on the stairs. I gave her a wink and dangled the transparent bag which was bulging with magic dust.

Once again I wiped down the cistern and lined up two London to Liverpool's. I call them this because they're as long as the rail track from London to Liverpool, get me? I then pulled out a crisp fifty and rolled it up.

"After you darling," I insisted.

Bazookas took the note and leaned over the toilet with her head low then snorted the whole lines in one go. She had a short cropped top on and hot pants which revealed the lovely curves of her body and showed me how mint her little ass was.

She stood up straight and looked around and caught me staring at her ass.

"Your turn," she said, handing me the rolled note.

I put the note to my nose, bent over and demolished my medicine. She grabbed my arse and squoze it gently.

"Nice arse," she said.

Within seconds her top came up and I buried my head in her huge space hoppers. She not only had a wicked tit job but also had both nipples pierced. I sucked both of them and Mr. wiggly woke up from his sleeping bag.

'Zip lob in yer gob.'

And she chomped away like she'd never been fed. The tit wank was first class and I could have stayed in there the rest of the night it was so good, but a few minuets later the cubicle door received a few hard bangs.

'BUMP, BUMP, BUMP.'

"How long you gonna be in there?" a desperate to piss sounding girl shouted.

I pulled up my trousers and she down her top.

"You go first," I said, "and I'll meet you next door."

She slid out the door and as I was just about to do the same a head appeared through the side of the door.

"Got any of that left for me?"

It was Lucinda, the Pammy look-alike from the stairs.

I pulled my shirt over my trousers so she couldn't see I'd got the raving hard on, but I think she clocked it first. 'Fuck it anyway' I thought, after the line that I'd just snorted had hit me I would of stood there bollock naked and not have given a toss. I felt like a dog with ten dicks.

Another London to Liverpool went down and whilst she was sniffing she deliberately waggled her backend and said.

"Go on then 'do' me."

I couldn't believe my luck. I banged her so hard and fast that both of her arms were up against the walls stopping her face from getting squashed against the tiles. The amount of moaning she was doing the whole of the women's toilets must have thought we were having a fight.

After we'd finished our business we walked out of the toilets looking like we'd been dragged out of a hedge backwards.

"Dirty bastards," shouted one fat, moustached hippo looking minger as we left.

"Fuck off you slaaag, you look like a truck driver," I shouted back giving her the finger.

Stana was five meters from the toilet entrance in Ethos and just stood there with one hand on his forehead and the other on his stomach, creased with laughter.

"Stan you ain't going to believe this mate," I told him, "It must be happy hour here because I've just had two for the price of one!" I added grabbing a bottle of water from off the table and tipping some of it into my hands flattening my hair back.

"Hi Shaney, how are you?"

Rachel and Becky, a couple of girls who we used to party with sometimes back then appeared.

"Alright girls, what are you up to?"

"Have you been naughty again in the women's toilets?" Rachel said.

"Me, what d'you mean. You know I'm an angel, I don't do things like that?" I replied sarcastically.

"We're going in about ten minutes if you want a lift home."

"Ok, I'll meet you outside then at one." I replied.

It wasn't much longer until the club closed anyway so Stana and I had a little nose around and finished off our drinks.

"Right then mate I'm off. Tell Hort that I'll see him tomorrow if you can pull him down from the ceiling." I added.

"Ok bro," Stan replied." Good luck with the hat trick," he added with three fingers in the air.

I stood at the top of the steps outside of the club and sparked up a Marlboro light. There were around forty people outside hanging around, most of them still 'off their cakes', heads still nodding even though there was no music to be heard.

Because there were two main entrances, One for Ethos and the other for the Zone I wasn't quite sure which side to wait as the distance between the two must have been twenty meters. There were chromed rails which ran across the full length of the three, four feet high walls outside to stop the customers falling over the edge .The bright pink and blue neon's which were advertising the clubs names lit up the huge car park with electric colours. I opened my mouth as wide as I could and moved my jaw from side to side as if I was yawning. It felt like all the muscles in my face had tightened and needed a little stretch to loosen them up. My right hand was in my pocket fumbling around to see how much money was left. I pulled out a handful of change and discovered the 'Californian sunrise' which I had left from the ten we'd got earlier. They were quite good these ones and gave you the 'rush of the century' as Hort used to say. I'd still got lines worth of charley in the plastic bag so decided to pop the pill inside, crush them both together, shake up the bag and make a nice mix. Empting the bag onto the back of my hand I then snorted the whole lot up both nostrils; 'Bastard, did that make my nose burn.'

Rachel and Becky finally appeared from the Zone, and both gave out 'here we are waves.'

"Alright birds, I thought you said ten minutes?"

"We had to wait for our coats, and the bitch in the cloak room took ages to find them? Becky said. "The fucking slag, I hate her, she does it deliberately every time," she added.

I just grunted, the Californian sunrise mix had just battered fuck out of my head and made me feel charged as if a bolt of lightening had struck me. My eyes pinned back and jaw locked up solid.

They escorted me down the steps one of them either side of me with our arms linked.

"Come on then 'Shaney Ranger' lets go party," said Rachel.

She used to call me this because she reckoned I acted like a Power Ranger when I was 'off it'.

We started walking from the steps to the middle of the car park. I could hear music being played from an oncoming vehicle getting louder and louder until the volume stayed the same. I heard a few voices and shouts, but we took no notice, it was probably some piss-heads rowing or something which was normal in Bentley in the early hours.

"Hey! Girls," someone yelled.

We all turned around to see who it was.

Around fifteen meters away and to our left was a big green Toyota Land Cruiser parked with what I could make out had six or seven people inside. All of the windows wound down and eyes on us.

The passenger side door opened and a bloke about my height got out. I couldn't quite make out his face as the light was behind him but I could see he was much stockier than I was. As he walked towards us it I realised it was 'Mr. Italiano' from the 'moody posse' shoulders were still swinging.

"Hey girls, you want a lift home with us?"

"No, we're with Shane," said Rachel.

"Yeah, we're with Shane," confirmed Becky.

"What you doing with him?" he yelled back, "I think he's a joker. Come with us."

"Listen mate, the fucking girls are with me, ok?"

He stood there a few seconds then took a few steps forward. At this point he was about ten yards away. Looking to his left I noticed there were words being exchanged in the land cruiser. I had to make a decision fast because things could have got way out of hand. The drugs riddling through my body made the decision for me. I was unable to think rationally. If it did kick off though I was fucked no matter what, but to bottle it with a bird on each arm would have hammered my ego. I couldn't let this happen.

I tuned to Rachel and said under my breath quietly.

"If that cunt takes one more step, I'm gonna knock him clean fucking out.

A few more seconds passed and luckily enough he didn't step forward .He just walked back to the cruiser and shouted. "Your loss, not mine," flicking his hand towards us as he climbed back into the passenger seat.

The Land cruiser stood still for a while. I couldn't take my eyes off it for a second because for all I knew they could have pulled around the back of the car park and all gave me a kicking. I was alone.

We jumped into Rachel's blue Citroen Saxo and pulled off onto the slip road by the side of the Showcase Cinema to head home. My heart was pumping ten to the dozen with the adrenalin and drug mix that was riddling through my blood stream.

After staying up until nine o'clock the following morning I jumped in a taxi and headed for home.

As the taxi pulled outside I could see my dad throwing a wobbly on the driveway. He was supposed to have been at the hospital for an appointment and because I'd parked my Astra convertible right up the arse end of his car he was unable to get out because the hand brake had stuck on.

"I can't get the fucking hand brake off the car and I've got to be at the hospital in five minutes," he shouted.

The last thing you need coming down off a major pill ,booze and Charlie binge is someone screaming at you , so I just 'lost it.'

I walked to the back of the car, put my finger in the hole where the boot lock used to be before someone tried to rob it the week before and opened up the hatch. I then pulled out a six pound lump hammer, smashed all of the windows, jumped inside and releasing the handbrake, rolled back the car."Happy now?" I asked. "I'm off to fucking bed, good night."

At this time of morning, because we lived on a main road I had an audience of drivers open mouthed on their quiet trip to work.

THE BIGGER THE UP THE BIGGER THE DOWN

I was hoping that it was all a bad dream. It was 5.30pm when I'd opened my eyes. The jaw ache I had felt like Tyson had been at me and I was in a very very delicate state. Walking down the stairs with my brain banging against the side of my skull my hand gripped the front door lock and twisted it anticlockwise.

As it swung open, I felt a lump in my throat. The car looked like someone had set off twenty pounds of explosive from inside it. There was glass everywhere and to add to it all, the rain was pissing down. Slamming the door, I went back in to the house and sat down with a hot cup of coffee with six sugars in an attempt to liven up my thoughts.

By the time I'd found someone with all of the glass in stock the best of a month's wages had been spent. Maybe next time I wouldn't be parking so close to other peoples' cars.

FETCH THE COPPERS

The following week was a '999 night' which was held on the last Wednesday of every month for the emergency services Police, Ambulance and Fire crew at the Zone. We used to get complimentary tickets from some of the staff from the Manor hospital who used to drink in 'Bushwackers' occasionally.

These were good old nights with gangs and gangs of drunken nurses always up for it, good tunes and cheap, cheap drinks. The whole of the Zone ended up wasted on this night.

We turned up around ten thirty as Elvis had to be picked up from Old bury first which was a trip down the motor way. There were two new doormen working who tried to knock us back on entrance.

"Fuck off mate, what do you mean, not tonight?" I said, "We've got tickets," I told him.

Just as I spoke Steve Gitters, the manager walked into reception.

"Sorry lads, come in I'll get you a drink. These lot are ok," he told the extremely pissed off looking doormen who weren't happy that their decision had been overruled.

"Sorry bro, but we've been coming here since it's been open, get yourselves a drink."

He nodded and put his hand on my back as we walked through.

"No problem, we didn't know. Cheers for the drink anyway," He accepted.

The Zone was already heaving with loads of nurses gulping back as much wine and Bacardi as they could hold. The other good thing about these nights was that you could find out the faces of the local old bill. Not that I needed to like, I'm a good boy remember.

There was once a case of one plod being spiked with acid, which if you don't already know is LSD, a strong hallucinogenic.

We told him that all the people who were drinking in this club were on his case and information had been leaked that he was a rent boy and they believed him to be obsessed with other men. We also told him that he was going to be questioned about his background by some undercover officers who were present in the club, but we didn't know exactly where. The only thing we were able to tell him was that it was most likely to be in the toilets.

He stood in a dark corner of the room for six hours while we fed him water telling him it was vodka and lemonade. He promised to buy all of our drinks if we could spot who was spying on him.

By the end of the night he was in a real bad state, we'd took nearly a hundred and fifty quid off him and shortly after that he was escorted out for pissing up the wall because he was too paranoid to go to the Loo's.

All you could hear him screaming when they were asking him to leave was, "No, no don't touch me, don't touch me, I'm not really a rent boy, I've never been paid to have sex with a man, honestly, I couldn't go to the toilets because they're going to start interrogating me, please, please ask my friends over there, they'll tell you. Ask them go on!"

By this time, we'd all fucked off into next door because most of his friends who were old bill as well had started to ask our descriptions. Not that I thought he'd of stitched us up. If the truth had been known he'd have probably said that 'we were a bunch of ever so helpful chaps who'd been helping him track down the sex interrogators and, to buy us a drink if they bumped into us for being such jolly good sports!'

We pushed through the bar next-door and grabbed a few Buds.

Stana disappeared for about ten minutes and returned with twenty pills which had a $ sign on them.

"Good lad," I said, "I was going to say we could do with some 'supper'."

Straight away, I did a double drop and as always swilled it down with a freshly bought JD.

Elvis, Stana and Hort looked around.

"Are these any good Shane?" asked Elvis moving a pill around in his hand.

"Fuck knows," I replied, "But times ticking mate. The only way to do the job is to double drop because if one isn't strong enough you'll want another and we've only got another hour or so left, get me?"

"But what if they're proper proper strong?" he answered back.

"Well that just means that in twenty minuets I'm going to be twice as 'off it' as someone who just took one, then who's gonna be pissed off eh? Not me bro, that's for sure!"

"Go on Elvis get two down ya," Hort said, egging him on.

"Or are you err scared?" I added.

Stana started laughing knowing the procedure. We always used to say 'you aren't scared are you' to wind up the situation and most of the time then, it did work.

Elvis walked towards the dance floor pills and a drink in his hand.

We knew he wasn't going to double drop , but I think this time he did at least have one and put the other one away so we'd believe he did take the two. Hort double dropped and swiftly tugged a bag of pink champagne out from his pocket.

"Wet yer finger Shane and stick it in there."

Before he finished his sentence my finger was back in my mouth, face cringing at the foul tasting whizz I'd just consumed.

"Fuck me Hort, that's rotten!"

"It'll be rotten in a minute kid, you won't sleep for a week on this, its fucking rocket fuel," he told me.

We took a little walk around and bumped into Abbey Heath. Abbey was around fifty years old and when he was younger he used to be a proper riot, always having tear ups in the town. There weren't many people he wouldn't have had it off with either. I got on really well with him. Even until today, he still plays up when he gets the Pernod down him. He got himself nicked in the town centre having a fight some years back and had to go to court.

"Mr. Heath," the judge said, "Do you have anything to say before we conclude this case?"

"Yes, I fucking do, I m the hardest fucking man in Walsall, nobody fucks with Abbey heath, I'll kill every fucker who tries, this is all a load of bollocks this. I don't even know why I'm here!" he screamed. "You can all fuck off"

I think the last few sentences gave him a stretch for contempt of court, but to be honest he didn't give a flying fuck, he's murder.

We stood and chatted for a few minutes whilst Hort and the lads did a lap.

He was just in the middle of telling me about when he'd leathered six lads in the Tavern in the Town doing all the actions and nearly knocking a couple of the people out who were brave enough to listen, when Hort waved me over.

"I'm off Abbey," I told him "Hort's shouting me."

"Ok son," He said, "look after yourself."

I grabbed my drink from off the bar and walked around the right hand side of the dance floor.

"Shit, that's good stuff Hort, I feel fucked," I said shaking my head to refocus my thoughts.

"And me," agreed Hort, "it's that whizz or is it the pills? Oh, I don't know which one it is but it's having me right at it!"

The thing was with Hort, he could never (under the influence) make up his mind what was and what wasn't. We were in Tenerife the once and had scoffed fifteen E's each. Hort swore blind that they hadn't done anything to him, even though we were both completely wankered. We both sat on the wall in 'Veronicas strip'. He went off to the burger stand and bought a cheeseburger. After he'd taken three mouthfuls of it, his eyes started to roll.

"These cheeseburgers are the bollocks," he told me.

"What're you going on about Hort?"

"Fuck the pills, this cheese burger is sending me off my head."

At that, he ran as fast as he could to the hamburger stand pushed to the front of the cue and demanded that the man handed over all of the burgers on the hot plate.

A few minutes later he returned with eight cheeseburgers and swore that the more he ate the higher he became. He convinced me that much I ate two of the fuckers myself and threw them up twenty minutes later all over the bonnet of a cop car after swigging back some GHB.

Anyway, I looked to my left and saw Stana chatting to a few blokes close to the bay seating area by the DJ console.

As I walked over, I realised he was talking to the crew I'd met on the car park a few weeks before.

"Shane this is Jim, and this is Az, they're from…"

I shook Jims hand then Az's without saying a word we all smirked at each other as if to say we'd met before.

"How you doin' lads?" I said, "You haven't come to nick my birds again have you?"

"You're just greedy you are," replied Jim.

"Yeah," said Az, "Two at a time, you just looked like you needed a hand the other week that's all."

"Oh, right, I'll have to grab enough for all of us tonight then eh?"

"Sounds good to me, what we all drinking then I'll get the round in?" said Jim.

We all stayed together until the end of the night and strangely things went really well considering the car park conflict a few weeks earlier. I'd also found out later that two of the men who were in the Land cruiser had recently been released from Winson Green prison in Birmingham. They had capped a couple of lads with sawn off shotguns, and there was me largin' it on the car park with two birds, less than a tenner and a runny nose. Now that would have been interesting would it not? They also told me that they were convinced because of what had happened that night I'd brought a firm of lads in to straighten the conflict out, mostly referring to Elvis, as he was six feet six and built like a brick shit house!

We all had a good old laugh and joke about it later and found it quite amusing.

Jim informed me that before we'd actually met he used to hate seeing me strut my stuff around the Zone with all the girls chatting to me 'giving it the big un' as he used to tell Az . 'Look at that cunt over there. Who the fuck does he think he his? I'm gonna knock him fucking out' he'd often say in his pure Scottish accent. The story of how we all met still is told to this very day. This was the beginning of a very close relationship between us all and we stayed like proper brothers ever since.

C.P. TENERIFE II

I received a letter today, May 1st 2004, from the instruction court in Tenerife south which reads as follows:

Case number 3068, Aug 2003

With reference to the said case of forgery, fraud and international organised crime committed on the 12 of August 2003

We wish to send the above case to the Audiencia National (crown court) in Madrid and decline jurisdiction in Tenerife.

We class this type of crime as a major monetary offence and wish the charges to be changed to 'Forgery of currency' Fraud, smuggling of contraband and international organised crime.

We believe this group of criminals to be an organised international gang British, Argentineans, Hungarians who dedicate their time to the fabrication, programming of credit cards, currency and passports in order to gain large quantities of money and live a life of luxury in the South of Tenerife.

Everything in this case leads us to believe that the afore mentioned individuals also have connections in Gran Canaria, Madrid, Russia and other countries again dedicated to illicit activities in the form of smugglingcontraband tobacco.

In the best interests of the court we must let it be clear that the 'King of Spain's Imperial suite,' which is situated in the Villa Cortes Hotel in Playa de Las Americas alone costs 2000 Euros per night which is where Mr. Lloyd and Mr. Olivetti had been staying for some time before arrest.

With this information, we would request the following petition for the said offences.

Currency forgery8 to 14years

Fraud4 years

International organised crime2 years

Judge of court number 3 signed.

'That's 20 years if it all goes Pete Tong!'

I've been in here a year so far and was told this week that the courts haven't even closed our case yet.

In the Canary Islands, you are supposed to be under the law of Spain, but the judicial system is completely fucked up. You are guilty until proven innocent and if you're looking at six years or more they can keep you locked up on remand for four years before they even pull out your file. Even if your worst case scenario is 3 years, they have the power to hold you in the local penitentiary for up to 2 years before they even decide whether or not you're anything to do with the case at all.

A friend of mine Dutch man Rene Jansen has already been on remand in Tenerife II for 3 years 10 months and 2 weeks. He was telling me just the other day that when he gets to the 4 year mark if they haven't taken him to court the law says he has to be released.

A few days later, the screw or 'functionario' as they're called in 'Spicland' called him over the tannoy which is situated in the middle of the concrete jungle he'd been waiting in for nearly four years. Then, told him that his court day had arrived and was dated in a few weeks. Some head fuck that one mate; believe me this place is worse than anything you see on TV.

The prison is fucked.

The people are fucked

And only if you don't mind eating squid rings and black bean soup every fucking day would you like the food.

The Canarian penitentiary TF II is made up of nine wings or 'Modulos' as they call them. Mod one is observation, two and three are for remand prisoners, nine for women prisoners and the rest for hospital workers and sentenced. Inside each Mod' are two small wings with a small concrete yard about the size of a five a side football pitch .The wings are standard two stories high and were originally built for one person, but extra beds were fitted inside to accommodate two men. Unlike the UK prisons, there is no suicide netting, as the prisoners prefer hanging themselves or wrist slashing as an option to jumping here.

Three weeks ago someone in another Mod' was found with slashed wrists in his cell and was barely alive, after the infirmary had bandaged him up he was charged shortly after with attempted murder on himself and was given an extra six year sentence!

Believe it or not, that's the law here.

The concrete five a side sized pitch has four large steps going down to it in all directions. There is a tiny library at the top right hand side of the yard and pokey toilets which stink of stale warm piss and are matted with flies and the outside has overhead metal netting in the lower parts and is painted burgundy, blue and green.

Generally these prisons carry all walks of life, Canarians, Russians, Columbians, Moroccans, Bulgarians, Romanians, Africans, Americans, a few Germans and a handful of English. Mostly violent crimes and drug offences are common here with some big boy with up to half tonnes of cocaine.

Some Venezuelans had been swallowing sausage size pellets and been caught with x-ray at the airport for smuggling. Many a man had lost his life because the pellets had burst in their stomachs.

The law in Spain says that the maximum you can serve for any amount of hashish or marijuana is four years. So if you get caught with 5 kilos or 5000 kilos the most you can get is a 'four' which is probably the only thing you can be sure of because the rest of the sentences are fucking ridiculous!

An old Canarian man got just 6 years for raping a Downs syndrome girl who was 14 years old, but for possession of two credit cards and buying a cheap camcorder my Hungarian friend Joseph Csbi Csbi got 9 years.

That's the Spanish mentality for you.

A few months ago two East Germans came in here for an armed robbery, Henry and Randy were they're names. The pair of them together didn't have a brain cell, but Henry the 'brainier' of the two came home from work one afternoon from his landscape gardening job in the south of Tenerife with his month's wages, which was around 800 Euros. Randy told him that he was pissed off that he didn't have a job and said how bad he felt because he couldn't get money from anywhere to 'chip in'. Henry told him not to worry and they sat in the house smoking heroin together. After a few tokes on the gear, Randy came up with an idea.

"Let's rob a petrol station," he told Henry.

Randy was 5 feet 4inches tall and fat with long blonde hair, while Henry, was 6 feet 5 and thin as a rake.

They bought a toy pistol from the shop and set off to the main TF1 motorway in their battered old Seat Panda to find the nearest petrol station to hold up. As they came to the Cepsa station on their right hand side they prepared themselves and pulled in.

Driving onto the forecourt, Henry, (smacked out of his head) pulled the gun from his jacket and walked inside where the cashier was standing, while Randy stayed outside in the car.

"Give me all the money, this is a hold up," he said.

The woman cashier quickly complied and emptied the contents of the till into a plastic shopping bag which he snatched off her and ran outside to where his trusty getaway driver was waiting. He got in the car and they sped away (if it's possible to speed away in a Fiat Panda).

Two hundred metres down the road Henry opened the bag and found 120 Euros in notes and a handful of change. They were just approaching the roundabout in Guaza town some 300 meters away from the station when the car started to judder.

The daft cunts had just robbed one of the biggest petrol stations in Tenerife for 120 Euros, which is about 80 quid, and forgot to put any petrol in the getaway car.

Within seconds the police had surrounded them with 15 armed patrol cars and to add to it Randy had left a 3 gram bag of heroin in the ashtray, which alone in Tenerife you get a 5 year sentence for.

The pair of them were arrested for armed robbery and fast tracked to appear in court quickly.

The heroin never appeared in the whole case. The judge said that they didn't use a real gun and didn't complete the robbery because the car had run out of petrol. Both of them got 2 year suspended sentences and ended up doing 4 months in prison.

Now that's what I call justice!

The thing I could never understand about this job was that Henry had just picked up his wages (800 Euros). Randy was the one with no money, but Henry did the job and pulled the gun out on the cashier. He must have either been a really good friend or a complete and utter twat. I don't need to tell you which one, do I?

England have just beat Croatia 4 -2 and Italy got kicked out of the euro cup playing Bulgaria. All of the Spanish are keeping quiet as they were knocked out a long time ago. The screws are now giving the British a hard time in mod 2 'Hooligans' they call us!

NO BAIL JUST JAIL

On the 27th of May, my second bail application was entered into the court in Arona. My lawyer Alfonzo Delgado has asked for my freedom on medical grounds and because of the lack of evidence. In four weeks or so I should get a reply. I'm not going to hold my breath though. The facts are that I am definitely in the wrong country to be getting exited about the possibility of being released on bail. Let's see

BUTLINS 97

Early summer of 97 was a busy year as far as the party scene went 'We just didn't stop'
This was the year of 'Butlins fever.'
Hort had taken his son away for a weekend down south to Minehead and discovered that the Butlins resort needed a good seeing to.
One Friday afternoon we all packed up early and bungled into the back of a 944 Porsche turbo, Stana, Hort, Doug, Azum and yours truly.
Doug was a proper nutter and I got on really well with him. His appetite for LSD when he was younger at the first raves in 1988 was incredible.
We hadn't realized that the Porsche wasn't the most ideal car to be traveling in until we'd traveled the first 20 miles.
Hort was well over 6 feet tall, Doug wasn't much smaller and had shoulders as wide as the car. Then there was all of our clothes, drinks everywhere, spliffs being built, pills being dropped down the seats, Doug farting like a bull after a curry and to top it all off it was hot, real hot.
"Wind your window down Stan it's as hot as a brothel in here," Hort Said fanning himself with a magazine.
As he did so a hard gush of wind tornado'd through the car. Az was in mid build and his spliff tobacco, skunk and papers all blew in our faces. There was weed everywhere in our eyes, ears, hair and all over our clothes on the rear parcel shelf.
Stan looked around to see what all the commotion was about as the horn of a large articulated lorry sounded as we drifted from the fast lane into the slow cutting up the angry driver. You could see his arm waving out of the side window; fist clenched cussing the bollocks out of us for nearly running him off the road.

Doug pressed the button above the rear view mirror and the electric sun roof slid backwards and, with a bottle of vodka still in his hands, he then stood on the passenger seat with half his body out of the car lobbed his tool out and screamed back at the lorry driver who was now directly behind us.

"Come on then yer bastards, I'll fucking kill ya!"

At that he passed the bottle back into the car and started to piss out of the sunroof pointing upwards towards the middle of the lorry. I don't know how he did it but he managed not to spill a drop on the Porsche and you could see the lorry driver creased up in his cab through our rear window. It's not very often that you see a grown man pissing out the roof of a Porsche doing 95 mph down the M6 is it? Doug too, was a proper showman. This was definitely going to be a weekend to remember as we were only half way there and we'd already polished off two liters of Smirnoff and a two gram bag of base whiz.

It took us around two and a half hours to get to the complex and by this time we were all on our way. The windows on the Porsche were blacked out, so you were unable to how many of us were inside. This worked out well because we had to sneak in the three who were in the back. The receptionist had informed us earlier there were only two vacancies in the whole of the resort because this weekend was the famous '18 to 30s" reunions and they were fully booked. All of this was done over the phone and she'd given us a reference number to hand in at the gate.

We sat and watched a few cars drive in first of all to see if the gate security checked inside of the cars because we didn't want to fuck it up after we'd traveled so far. Lucky for us they didn't

Through the mesh fencing which covered the complete front entrance you could see hoards of people surrounding the mini fair which was lit up with millions of multicolored flashing lights, bumper cars, rockets, candy floss stall crowded with screaming kids and their parents. I'd always been a fair lover since I was a kid and I felt butter flies in my stomach, as I had a flash back of my childhood.

We pulled into the queue behind a family in a grey Volkswagen golf. At this point we were three cars away from the gate security cabin. We could see an old fat man with a bushy grey beard behind the counter pressing a red button to raise the electric barrier which allowed the car to pass through. The first car sailed through without problems which left the Volkswagen then us, no problems so far. Just when we thought everything was okay another man appeared from the side door of the cabin and started to walk in our direction.

"Shit I hope the twat don't start looking inside the cars," I cussed.

"Cover yourselves with the blanket on the back window lads the fucker coming over," Hort said.

The guard was standing on the curb as the golf drove through the raised barrier.

"Don't move an inch and keep quiet."

You could see the blanket twitching as the lads were sniggering like kids underneath. I tried to hold my smile as I jumped out of the car.

"Alright mate?" I said. Walking towards him while Stana pulled the car forwards. "We got a number here for you, 2435b. The lady on the telephone told us to give this to the handsome fellow on the gate. That must be you right?" I added.

"I don't know about that," he replied with a big smile. "I used to be handsome a few years back."

"Nah mate, it's definitely you, there's only you and Father Christmas pressing the button right?"

He chuckled once again and raised his hand to Father Christmas to press the button.

"Down to your right and first on your left, enjoy your stay," he told us, as I quickly jumped into the passenger seat and told him I'd buy him a drink when he'd finished work.

"Come on lets fuck off quick," I said, as the barrier lifted and we slid into the twilight zone.

I went into the reception with Hort to collect the keys. The huge car park to the right hand side was absolutely chocka.

"Fuck me Shane the car park was half this full last time and all the pubs were full to the brim," said Hort with a voice of excitement.

After around twenty minutes of emptying the car of clothes booze and everything else we arrived outside of the chalet. As the front door opened you could smell the holiday caravan smell which I remembered from all the holidays we took when we were kids.

Everyone started to put their clothes on hangers and claim their beds. The chalet they'd given us was easily capable of holding four comfortably. The bathroom was a little small, but other than that the 45 pound it'd cost was well spent.

Az was already in the shower. "Don't use all of the water bro," Stan said.

"I'm only having a quick one," he replied.

I've done this sort of thing before and can guarantee that by the time I get in the water will be fucking freezing.

Doug found the remote control for the TV. "Are there any porno's on?" he enquired.

"Fuck me Doug we're in Butlins not Amsterdam," I told him, as we all burst into laughter.

"I know that," he replied, "but they could of put a special showing of Debbie does Dallas for us eh?"

"Or champers shags Chicago ah?" added Az.

"Right Az I'm next in the shower," said Hort darting towards the bathroom.

I sat down for a while and pulled a bag of skunk from my jacket. "Any one brought any cigs with them?" I got no reply so put five papers together and filled them with just weed. We were all whizzing our tits of any how and needed a strong spliff to take the edge off the matter.

I sparked it up and took a long deep toke. With my feet up on the chair I grabbed the remote off Doug and scanned through the radio channels on the TV menu until I found a decent station with dance music. The volume was turned up high and the tunes started banging out. We all started dancing arms in the air, bouncing on the beds and screaming as loud as we could. Stan pulled out his bottle of JD and a two liter bottle of coke and lined up our favorite tipples.

The party had started.

An hour later we were all ready. The apartment looked like it had been robbed and we'd only been on the complex two hours. There was no booze left or whizz and we resembled mental institute escapees.

Doug was sitting in the corner of the chalet rocking backwards and forwards making strange noises.

"You ready Doug?"

"Yeah man, yeah, lets go," he replied.

A few sprays of aftershave later we were off.

"Someone had better remember where the chalet is, and the number," said Stana.

"It's easy man, five B, Redwood," mumbled Doug.

We took forty paces around the corner and I asked Doug again. "Err, its down there man."

Fuck me we were going to struggle later on. We'd brought forty pills with us called 'Disco biscuits' and guess who had been looking after them?

"Are those biscuits any good Doug," asked Az.

"Yeah man. The one proper. Here 'av' one man, 'av' one."

Doug put his hand down his pants and pulled out a plastic zippy bag full to the brim of big brown colored pills and after a few seconds of fumbling to find the split at the top of the bag it popped open.

"Take two each man I've already had two earlier when we were getting ready," he told us. Proper dead trippy they are, all mad colours and that man," he added.

Doug was completely of his head. This explained why he'd been rocking backwards and forwards in the chair earlier.

I double dropped straight away not allowing Doug to have all the fun and the other all followed suit.

The complex in Minehead was huge. It must have seated 20,000 people. There was a massive dining hall, indoor and outdoor pool, a boating lake and five huge clubhouses with various themes to them. As we got closer to the centre which took us twenty minutes to get to, we noticed an indoor super market and we all piled in.

"No way," I shouted.

"What you found Shane?" said Hort bowling over to where I was.

"Look Hort, they sell mad dog 20/20 here I can't believe it, I told him happy to see the fruity flavoured, high octaned juice that is usually only on sale in the off licenses in Walsall. I quickly grabbed half a litre of strawberry flavour, whipped of the top and downed the lot. Hort followed then Doug and Az. I looked down to my right and saw that the cashier was way too busy serving other customers to notice we were doing anything and at that hid the empties behind the fridge and opened another five sinking them straight away.

"Alright birds, what you drinking?" I asked, pulling three diamond whites from the fridge, I popped the lids off with my teeth and passed them to the girls who'd just walked in.

"You'll have to drink 'em here standing next to the fridge ladies," said Hort.

They drank them, said thank you, and left.

We must have been in the super market forty five minuets. There was no mad dog left, no diamond whites and the back of the fridge looked like a bottle bin.

"Come on lads lets fuck off," Az said.

"Hang on where's Doug?" Hort asked, with a frown.

Doug came walking around the corner with one of those transparent cake trays in his hand from out of the fridge.

"Doug you can't tell me you're fucking hungry after all those drugs you've necked?"

"Nah man, I'll put it back then eh?" he replied.

He walked away and as far as we knew had put it back where he'd found it in the refrigerator. We got to the check out and bought sixty Marlboro lights.

"Excuse me love," said Hort. "You haven't got much booze in stock have you?"

The girl looked up from the till with a slightly confused expression on her face and didn't say a word. I kicked Horts shoe as if to say 'shut up', but he just burst into raging laughter and his face turned blood red as he bent over holding his stomach.

"Come on Doug." he was dragging behind us mumbling something and then laughing to himself half spitting at the same time. The double drop I'd taken earlier was starting to take its toll, the walls started bending and everyone sounded like cartoon characters. Stan's face said it all. His chin had started to stick out and grind from side to side like Jimmy hill on a bender. We all staggered out of the archway where the shops and supermarket were and walked left. There was an Irish bar at the side of the exit which looked quite busy. We could hear lots of girls screaming and shouting from the outside, this looked like our sort of place to start off with.

It was a typical Irish theme bar with bare wooden floors, walls and ceilings covered with instruments and bric a brac. The floor was plastered in loose wood shavings and cricket bats were hanging above the bars.

"Is it going to kick off in here Shane or what?"

Doug was tripping badly. His face was red and his hair was soaked where he'd been dripping with sweat.

"No Doug mate don't worry, were just off our heads that's all, relax a bit".I told him.

"What about the cakes man, the cakes are following us man. Oh man, Shane what we gonna do man?"

I looked over towards the door and there was jam donut standing there with a dickey bow on. Maybe he was right, the cakes were following us, but what had we done to them? I'd never even spoken to a cake before, especially one with a dickey bow on.

Doug latched on to the worried look on my face and turned his head around quickly towards the door. "What's up Shane, what's up?"

"Nothing is up mate. I told you it's just those pills making us all hallucinate."

Hort came over then Az and Stana.

"Hort listen," I said. "Doug is tripping his bollocks off big time. Help me calm him down a bit mate."

"You alright Doug," asked Hort.

"Yeah man, proper Hort, proper," replied Doug.

Hort got the round in and we all sat down by the window. I was too scared to look back at the door again in case the donut was still there and after all I was the one trying to calm Doug down. If I was to ask anyone if they could see a cake standing on the front door I would of looked a right twat.

"Hort, this is going to sound raving mad, but can you see that cake standing on the door with a bow tie on?

"Fucking hell Shane, have they got you as well?"

"Has who got me?"

"The pills"

"Oh yeah, tripping like a fucker me," I told him.

"And I am," he said with relief.

"What can you see then?" I asked him.

"All the trumpets on the wall keep spinning around and playing on their own."

"There's something going on over here as well bro," Az added.

Stana was sitting there with glazed eyes which were fixed on the back wall.

"Stan, you ok mate?"

"Stana" His eyes closed and head shook from side to side.

"Fucking hell, I was off with the fairies then," he said like he just had a coin put in his meter.

"I'm not having any more of them pills mate."

"Stana, you're a lightweight," I said. "You've got nothing to worry about, we're all looking after each other here. Don't fight it just ride the waves," I told him.

"I'm trying Champers, but it's fucking difficult to try and ride the waves when the whole of the pub looks like the cast of the magic roundabout!"

"I must be 'Dougle' then," mumbled Doug, with a small burst of giggling.

Everyone started to overheat. There was no air conditioning in the bar and the more people that came in the hotter it became.

Az popped to the toilets to wash his face with cold water and Hort followed him. While Az was gone we crushed up two pills and put them in his half drunk pint of larger. Swilling them around and trying to dissolve them before he came back. Doug had started to rock back and forwards again, talking to himself with both eyes closed.

The barmaid came over to collect glasses from the tables with an Irish Rugby shirt on which doubled as a dress. She had long blonde hair which nearly touched her ass and black high heeled shoes. Her feet were covered in plasters which were hiding the blisters she'd accumulated over the past several days work. Other than that she looked quite tasty compared to the rest of the staff. She got to our table and started to pick up a few of the twenty or so empty glasses which were cluttering up space.

"Is your friend ok," she politely asked, as she wiped down Doug's side of the table with a beer towel.

"Yes darling he's fine. He's an ex Vietnam veteran suffering from post pneumatic stress disorder. Rumor has it that he took out a whole section of two hundred and fifty troops single handedly after being subjected to torture for forty days and forty nights in the jungle."

"Your off your head you are," she said, quite amused at my verbal diarrhea

"Pleased to meet you .I'm Champers and you are…?"

"Karen"

I reached out my hand and dropped a pill in her palm as we shook.

I asked her where the best places to go were and she told me that there was a late night club opened called 'Hurricane Harrys', this was where all of the
Workers went after they'd finished their shifts.

"See you there after twelve," she said, and thanked me for the gift assuring me that she'd take it later.

"No problem," I replied.

As she left to collect up the rest of the empties from the now heaving bar a group of fifteen lads staggered in through the front doors. I think they must have been rugby players as a few of them had navy blue blazers on with badges on the breast pockets. Within minutes they had started to bother some of the girls who had been standing up the bar since we'd arrived. Most of them were short and stocky with shaven heads, shouting and spilling beer all over the sawdust covered floorboards as they ranted on in their own language.

Six of the group moved over to where our table was slamming their glasses of bitter down in a rude and irritating manner. They were welsh rugby players id realized getting a closer look at the badges.

Az started to make sheep noises as he walked in pushing through the six of them.

"Baaaaah, Baaaaaahh."

Doug came out of his coma and started laughing as all six of them turned and looked at our table.

"Alright lads?" said Az, "Bit hot in here with those jackets on innit?"

If looks could kill we would have died instantly. I'm not quite sure whether they were stunned by what had just been said to them or, they just couldn't work out which planet we were from by the disfigured looks on our faces.

Az could have a row, and without a shadow of a doubt he had the front to go with it. Doug was a complete nutter and Hort and I both had 500,000 volt stun guns down our socks and a can of CS gas each.

"Not 'WOOL' are they, those coats you're wearing?"

Azum couldn't help himself when he was 'off it', he liked playing turf wars, especially on foreign grounds when no one knew who was who, it gave him a buzz.

"Are you taking the piss mate?" said the fattest one of the two.

"Naaaaah mate, course not. We thought you looked a little hot with those sheep jackets on OK?" I said.

"So fuck off you prick" Doug shouted, hands shaking.

Fat boy looked up the bar towards his friends, who were slobbering over some old rough looking women. They weren't gonna do much. The majority of them was struggling to stand and didn't even notice all of the commotion that was going on only feet away.

Fat boy grabbed a drink from the table and knocked it back in one. His five friends' didn't say a single word and tried their best to avoid eye contact, looking at the floor in retreat.

We all sat back down eyes still fixed on the sheep shaggers in case they decided to attempt a surprise attack.

"Which ones my drink?" said Az with a big smirk on his face.

"Shit, that fat cunts just knocked your drink back with two crushed up pills in it," I said.

That'll teach him. He won't know what's hit him in twenty minutes," Come on let's go somewhere else," Doug pleaded, finishing off his drink

We pushed through the sweaty crowds 'dead eyeing' the woolies on the way out. It was nice and cool outside and the doormen had stopped being donuts and changed back into white shirts.

"Keep an eye on that gang of Welsh lads at the bar mate, they just asked us if we wanted to buy heroin," said Doug.

"Yeah, the fat one with the bald heads got a knife as well" I said, "I thought Butlins was for families not junkies?"

"Cheers lads," thanked the doormen as we walked away.

Within seconds of us leaving, the doormen were on there radios calling for back up to the bar. As two of them passed us we shouted, "Hurry up lads, one of them had a knife,"

The security looked a little worried. If you could imagine what they were thinking on the way there, that twelve big Welsh heroin dealers were kicking off on their complex with knives .

When they were at the job center for an interview as security, the women at the desk must have said, "Its not a real strenuous job, the majority of the people are families and children so you're not going to be 'fighting' with anyone at Butlins!"

Doug pulled out his bag of tricks and we all had another pill each.

Even Stana had one after a bit of persuasion. I chewed mine for a quicker hit.

Smack in the middle of the fairground was one of those horseracing games where you have to throw the balls in the holes to make the horses cross the finish line first. The one at the top is red and your horse moves three times if you throw the ball in it. The blues two and the three yellow holes gave you one move. Usually each person gets three balls to throw at any one time. We all paid our 50p each and were under starters orders.

'And they're off......'

Hort took the lead first by throwing a three with Az up close behind, then Stan over took with a four. I moved up into second place. Doug threw a six and over took me then got really excited and decided to rob three more balls from another lane which wasn't being used. He was so wrecked he had forgotten which lane he'd started in and ended up throwing six balls down an alley which wasn't even switched on. Hort threw a ball at Stana. I threw two at Doug. Doug threw six balls at the old women behind the counter, and I followed with another four, bang on the forehead.

After the game, Doug went around the back to apologize to the lady whilst Az robbed all the money from out of the till!

"Good old Butlins" Az shouted.

We decided to take a little walkabout and found Hurricane Harrys. It didn't open until late we thought it would be better to locate it now rather than later.

Hort had a piss in the letter box at the side of the building. I don't know whether he thought it would make it easier to find later, so I pissed in it as well. You never know animal instinct and all that.

'Harrys' looked quite big from the outside. It had a moat around the entire building and you had to cross a large wooden bridge to get to the front doors. At the side of Harrys was a huge club house called Barnum's. This was where usually all the main stage shows were for families, cabaret, karaoke and games for the kids. This place alone must have held 3000 people.

The last of the pills we'd scoffed gave me a 'come-upance' I could feel my balance start to go wonky as we walked towards the wooden picnic benches in an open area, not far away from the indoor swimming pool.

We sat down and drank the rest of the diamond whites we'd robbed from the supermarket earlier while Az built a spliff.

"Which club shall we go in first then Shane?" asked Hort, as he eyed up three mini skirt clad girls who were passing by us.

"Don't know Hort were spoilt for choice tonight mate. We've got the Ibiza foam party in Barnum's, Aya Napa reunion in the wagon wheel and about three or four other reunions at the other places.

"Ibiza foam party means girls in bikinis though eh?"

"Yeah, foam party sounds the one," Az agreed.

I sparked up the spliff and passed it to Az.

"I think Az is right you know. I reckon we should all do a pub crawl first, grab a few JD's in each place and chat up a few ladies. Then we can all fuck off to the foam party and finish off in Hurricane Harrys. We all agreed on our plan of action but needed to sit and absorb a touch of the cold breeze that was blowing outside before we made a move.

Doug's eyes had started to roll, Az went as red as a beetroot and Stana was shaking like a leaf. To add to that, I felt like I was cooking from the inside out and kept forgetting where I was and who I was with. The people that were walking past our table had just become a blur of colours and sounds and not making any sense at all. My eyes were flickering and my whole body leant to the left until I had nearly fallen off my seat. We sat there until it was nearly dark watching the bright lights of the fair flashing madly with lasers crossing the skies like something off star wars.

"Man this is freaky," Doug said.

For a few seconds my mind had convinced me that I was on the streets of Las Vegas with a ten gallon hat on and a big Cadillac convertible. Eventually, we peeled ourselves from off the bench and headed towards the wagon wheel where the Greece reunion was being held. As we got closer we got our first glimpse of the thousand or so people dressed in togas and mad shit. Either side of the huge doors which led you into partyville stood two eight feet high statues dressed up like Romans with green leaved crowns on top of their heads.

"Can I see your key rings please lads," Said one of the door securities.

"Shit" I'd noticed that they were checking over the radios to see how many people lived in each chalet, which meant 'legally' we would be able to get in two of us.

Hort and Doug went inside first and we waited for them to go into the toilets, and drop the key ring through the window which was situated at the right hand side of the building.

Within half an hour we were in the queue and with a little trickery eventually got in to find that Hort was hypnotizing six girls with his mating dance, pissing of sweat with two drinks in his hand.

Realizing that they were real players I joined in and soon pulled one away from the pack and took her to a quieter part of the club to play.

"You remind me of Robbie Williams", she informed me while I lifted up her toga and shoved a Lamot pills bottle up her fanny. She turned out to be a good old girl did Georgina, if only all girls were like her. I also had a funny feeling that she was a 'lettuce licker' as well because she seemed to be spending quite a lot of time feeling her mates arse nevertheless, I couldn't get her to do the show. After spending a little more time with her I had decided that she was costing me a small fortune in bottled beers so I decided to get off.

Hort was bang at it up the bandit doing one of those mad sloppy kisses that you used to do behind the bike sheds at school when you eat each other and come out with red lipstick all over your faces.

"Enjoying yourself Hort?"

"Have a feel of her tits Shane"

He was right they were proper and after seeing me she came up with the idea to swap, good girl.

"There you go Hort this is Georgina, she gets through a few drinks, but she's a player ain't you darling?" I said squeezing her arse.

She gave Hort one of those faces looking up with her chin pushing down onto her chest and a straw sticking out of the fishy pils bottle between her baps.

All four of us agreed and swap we did the other girl sucked cock like a pornstar, she did the motorbike, corn on the cob, licking the stamp, everything. The moment we'd left them they were back up the bar doing exactly the same with another group of lads and were just out for the play up like we were.

Az had found some lads who wanted to swap some sniff for pills and, after a little tester the deal was done.

Back up the bar a big fat Geordie lad was shouting his mouth off saying that someone had robbed his drink and from nowhere I appeared with a fresh piss and lager shandy and gave it to him to calm him down. He shook my hand and said "Cheers man," in a broad Geordie accent.

I smiled back and told him it was my pleasure.

On the way out of the wheel Doug had picked two pissed lads pockets so we'd now got enough key rings to get inside the next club. We made our way out of the main exit thanking the doormen on our departure.

The fair had started to close down but you could see at this point that the whole of this complex was rammed inside and out of crazy 18 to 30 party goers.

On the dance floor of Barnum's we bumped into a few girls who recognized us from our last trip to Tenerife where Hort had discovered his 'Ecstasy burgers' in Las Veronicas. I couldn't really remember them but they told us we'd dropped them off in our jeep with no money or idea where they were staying. It took them seven hours to get to the Police station to get help. After they'd been ranting on for a short while I slid away I thought they looked like they were about to put a compensation claim in.

I walked around the edge of the dance floor looking for a cigarette machine but they were all empty. I decided to try the supermarket and told everyone to stay where they were for a while. Luckily one of the workers had told me that the supermarket was open and as I pushed through the dark blue swinging doors to get out of Barnum's I noticed there was someone coming through at the same time. It was the sheep shagger from the Irish bar earlier who'd been giving it the 'big un'. He put his arms around me and kissed me on the side of the head.

"I don't want any trouble. I love everybody and everybody loves me," he said dropping to his knees with his hands together looking like he was about to pray. "I went to the toilets after you'd left and fell asleep on the toilet. When I woke up half an hour later my head felt like it was going to explode so I put it under the tap to cool down and went back inside the bar to look for my friends. It took me an hour and a half to realize they'd been thrown out."

"Well where are they then?" I asked him.

"Fuck knows, the gang of girls at the bar told me loads of security turned up and told them if they didn't leave the complex the police would be called."

"What the fuck were you doing then wooly bollocks, selling drugs or something eh?"

"Funny you should say that. They reckoned we'd been selling heroin and flashing kitchen knives at their customers." He told me.

"You don't look the sort kidda to be honest. I thought you were more like a happy go lucky type of bloke who likes a few beers. You surprise me, but I suppose they come in all shapes and sizes theses days."

"I am mate, but the problem is I'm fucked now. How am I supposed to get back to Wales on Sunday? I've got to be at work at eight o'clock Monday morning and I think someone put something in my drink because I'm hallucinating badly."

"No shit," I said, "what can you see?"

"Well its going to sound really bad, but I went to the toilets in a bar half hour ago bursting for a piss. I pushed open the door and looked in the mirror. My faced looked a little weird and my eyes had gone really big."

I knew he was getting to the best bit as he was holding on to my trouser leg at this point and his face looked rather distressed.

"Loose my trousers you fat cunt. It looks like you're begging for a tin of fucking chappy. Get up," I shouted.

"Sorry mate, sorry"

"That's better, now carry on. The toilets?"

"Yeah, I turned around and walked along the wall that you have a piss up. I zipped down my flies and my dick had disappeared."

"What, you trying to say Wooly, someone robbed it?" I asked him sarcastically. "Or maybe you could have left it at the chalet? Have you checked your pockets?" I added.

He started to pat the front and back of his trousers, then he tried his shirt pocket. I was trying my best not to burst into laughter, biting my bottom lip as I watched him looking around as if he'd lost a bunch of keys.

"Fucking hell. What're you going to do now Wooly?"

"No car"

"No mates"

"And your cock's been nicked. Fucking hell, I hope you had a tracker on it?" I said, shaking my head from side to side as if to say 'I don't know'. His head dropped and his lips disappeared inside his mouth, the heel of his palm was the only thing stopping his head going any further to the floor as 'I can't believe this is happening to me' was traveling through his head.

"Listen wooly, I'm going to be back here in ten minutes. I've just go to go see someone about something ok?" I told him as his head lifted back up and his face changed into a dog's who'd just been promised a walk.

The thing was I knew deep down that this bloke was a proper horrible cunt and if he hadn't of accidentally drank the lager and disco biscuit cocktail that we'd made for Az earlier. Without a doubt he would have been driving up the M6 to 'Woolyland', wondering why he'd been launched out of Butlins with the rest of the heard, you get me? I needed to teach this one a proper lesson and have lots of fun doing so. Besides that he owed us the 'dollar' for two pills already the cheeky cunt!

"Alright darling?" They'd changed the girl at the supermarket to a mid thirties brunette. "Is this a 24 hour shop?" I asked.

"NO we close at 4.30 am and re open at 8.30am" she informed me.

"Ok, cool" I said, scanning the isle for something to cause a mischief.

I bought sixty cigs and went on my way.

As I walked out of the front doors I noticed that the 'Spice girls' were standing outside with cans of Pepsi in their hands.

"Alright birds?" I said, winking as I passed by them.

Two girls who were sitting opposite eating sandwiches started laughing and then muttered amongst themselves.

'How cool am I?" I thought, to pass the Spice girls, drop them a wink and Stroll on. I looked back at them again and realized they were Pepsi promotion cardboard cut outs. Milliseconds later I had a brain wave.

I needed to hold the title for the only man in existence to take all of the Spice girls back to his gaff at the same time. It's the only way forward I thought. Sparking up a Marlboro light, I stood and thought of the best way to kidnap them without anyone screaming 'Fetch the coppers!' Should I go and get wooly and tell him to be look out? Nah, he was too fucked for anything, and if the truth be known the prick would of probably grassed me up after the goings on in the bar earlier. Time was ticking and it stood a good chance that the brunette in the shop would be closing up soon, it needed to be now so I walked over to the two girls who'd been amused to see me leaving the shop earlier.

"Listen girl's I've got a proposition for you"

They both swayed backwards as if I was about to rob their handbags.

"I'm going to give you ten pounds for free if you can go in the shop, tell the lady that you can't find the salt and vinegar Pringles and ask her to show you where they are, even if you can see them ok?" I asked.

They looked at each other as I pulled out a twenty pound note. I'd meant ten between them, but seeing the looks on their faces thinking they were getting one each told me that's what they needed to do a proper job.

"I don't want to know your names and if you see me again tonight you must promise to act like you've never seen me before in your lives ok, promise?"

They nodded their heads and I turned to walk away.

"Right, when I say go, go."

The supermarket was on the left hand side of the indoor archway with a shoe shop just to its right. I hid in the doorway.

"Ready?"

"Go"

They left their empty sandwich trays on the seat and walked towards the entrance, wiping their hands clean with serviettes.

I put my head to the edge of the wall to try to listen to them telling the shopkeeper what they couldn't find.

"Hello, can you show us where the salt and vinegar Pringles are please?" one of the girls said.

"They're just over there in the far right corner, second shelf down," replied the till girl.

There was a silence for around ten seconds a more distant voice shouted.

"I can't find them. Where about are they?"

I heard the counter door go up and then bang back down indicating that she'd left and gone to show the girls where the Pringles were.

Keeping close to the wall I peeped around the corner to see how far away they were. There was no one in sight. 'Right lets go.'

I sped straight to them and grabbed Ginger, Posh, Baby and Sporty. For some strange reason Scary wasn't connected to the rest of the group and stood alone as a separate cut out. I ran as fast as I could towards the bottom of the archway with all but Scary spice in my arms. Hiding them face up underneath a static caravan (sorry birds) I flew back down the arch way in pursuit of Mel B hoping that I still had the girls chatting to the shopkeeper in the supermarket to divert her away from the kidnappings.

When I got there and saw they were at the till my heart missed a beat, but they hadn't seemed to notice that anything had gone on, so I grabbed Scary and fled back to the others panting and nearly falling over in the desperate struggle to get away.

After re-uniting the group I made sure that they were all hidden away safely and started to make my way back to Barnum's past the supermarket. Everything was normal, no problem.

The till girl, was still sitting at the counter in the same position as if nothing had happened.

Job done!

The two girls who'd done an excellent divert must have walked out of the other end of the archway also realizing it was 'mission accomplished'

I made my way past the candy floss van and hook a duck stalls glancing up and smiling at the horse racing stand which had been raided earlier.

Finally, I reached Barnum's. I passed the doorman who I had told earlier I was off to buy some fags, gave him a nod and started to walk up the huge bending flight of stairs where Wooly was still at the top chatting to some oldish women who looked like a school dinner lady.

"This you're new bird wooly?"

He was all teeth and smiles. She turned around and smiled showing me that she'd only got two teeth at the bottom and one at the top.

"Hello Smiler, what's your name then?" I asked her.

"Don't take the fucking piss outta me!" she growled back.

"Fuck me, chill darling. My good friend Wooly here had told me before I'd left that he'd been eyeing you up some time earlier and he thinks you're a right tasty number. Isn't that right Wooly?"

Wooly looked at me with total confusion written across his face. I'm sure that by his expression and considering his state that he didn't even know this girl was a 'class A' bruiser. Just for the wind up as I passed her, I pinched her gargantuan arse and Wooly received a very hard slap across the face.

"Keep your dirty hands to yourself Wooly, this young lady is respectable aren't you sweetheart?" I told him.

"Yes I fucking am you dirty cunt, so keep your fucking hands to yourself, I'm not a slag you know like all the others!" she snapped as Wooly's bottom lip quivered.

"See Wooly, you dirty twat. All the fucking same you Welsh cunts. Grabbing goods you don't own." I said.

"Anyway darling he's no good to no fucker him, he's just been telling me that somebody robbed his tadger."

The old girl gave off a hideous laugh which sounded like the wicked witch of the west from 'The wizard of Oz.' then she walked off.

Wooly started to take short hard breaths then stormed off into the club.

Inside, the lads were in full swing. Hort and Azum were both on the podiums giving it loads. Doug was standing in the middle of the dance floor nodding his head up and down and as usual standing up the bar was Stana talking some poor bloke to death who probably thought he was Portuguese he was talking so fast.

Since we'd started going to the Zone Stan had grown his hair into a pony tail and when he'd popped too many pills you could either find him chatting at the speed of light or bouncing up and down on the dance floor with a 'Captain cave man' hair do.

"Stan"

"Stan"

"Stana"

I was standing in front of him yelling, but it was as if I wasn't there. I poked him in the ribs and he turned around and looked at me with a mad pill face grin.

"I've just seen that Welsh twat by the main entrance door and he's absolutely fucked mate. He told me that the entire wooly herd just got chucked of the complex for selling brown and they'd left the mouthy twat fast asleep on the karzie!" I said.

"Where is he now?" Stan asked gurning like a fucker.

"I don't know, some fat witch just twatted him across the head on the stairs and he fucked off."

The lad who Stan had been talking to looked pale and drained. "You ok mate? I'm Shane pleased to meet you."

"My name's Jason from Newcastle, What's yer pal been eating like, he's been yakking loads of bollox to me man for the last 45 minutes?" he went on to tell me. "I haven't been able to get a word in edgeways with him man."

"Too much sun and vitamins mate," I said.

Stana tried to start another conversation with him and Jason walked off to one of the seated areas to the right hand side of the building to escape a perforated eardrum.

Eventually I peeled him away from the bar and we started to make our way to the dance floor. I had to keep turning around every few paces in case he pounced on another victim. Stana had definitely got more rabbit than Sainsbury's. Maybe it would have been a better and cheaper idea for me to have used him to divert the shopkeeper. In fact I could have emptied the whole fucking supermarket, till, fridges and the shoe shop next door without going noticed!

I tried to explain what had happened to me earlier as we were pushing through the busy crowds of party animals, but like a Chinese whisper it had all been blown out of proportion by the time we got to the middle where Doug was.

"Doug, Doug." Stan said. "Shane's pulled five tasty girls and they're all waiting under our caravan with spicy Pringles," he added.

"Ehh?" mumbled Doug, his head exploding with all the information Stan had just rammed into it.

Az and Hort appeared and we all walked towards the entrance where it was a little quieter.

"What did you do that for Shane?" asked Hort, with a face as serious as cancer.

"Done what, Hort?"

"That's not like you bro" Az added.

"Hang on, hang on what the fuck you all going on about?" I asked them.

"Doug's just told us that you broke into a caravan, ran away with five girls and one of them had got 'shingles'." Hort said.

"No, you daft fuckers, I said to Stan that I just got two girls to divert the shopkeeper with a box of Pringles so that I could kidnap the Spice girls!"

Now they were all completely confused, and after thinking about it myself for a few seconds, I too wasn't quite sure and said no more about it. The lads stood there scratching their heads.

"Right then let's go to the foam party," I said, marching off towards the bright lights of the Ibiza reunion.

Now this had to be fun, I thought, as we all piled into the toilets at Barnum's and polished off the rest of the Charlie and necked a pill chaser just because we could. The security wouldn't allow you to take your drinks from venue to venue so we all put the drinks into our pockets and snook out through one of the fire exits, which by coincidence, brought us next to Hurricane Harrys.

"Fuck me, Hort you were right about pissing in the letter box mate. I'll have to remember that one in the future." I said smirking.

"Strange innit that?" Stana had tried to convince himself we really did end up there because of the smell of the piss. "My dog always does that," he added.

"You trying to tell me your dog pisses in night club letter boxes Stan? I've seen him, he's a Yorkshire terrier, if that's the case then he's either got a ten foot cock or he wears high heels!" We all broke out into laughter except Stan who really had lost the plot for the moment. His hand pushed against his forehead then swept back his hair.

"Don't worry mate, just think about those spicy Pringles we've got waiting for us waiting back at the chalet," Az said.

Outside the club there was a huge banner about sixty feet long with the words 'Club 18 to 30's Ibiza foam party' written across it in big gold lettering. Now this did look impressive. On the roof, they had a super trooper revolving projector, which splattered images across the dark night's sky and looked really cool.

There were two 'A' boards either side of the doors, painted with big gold lettering explaining 'No drinks on the dance floor,' And

'Anyone found consuming illegal substances on the premises would be removed'

"Removed to where, the fucking bar?" I said.

First of all, you were six feet in foam so how will any fucker see you've got a drink in your hand, and secondly, the security on the front door were over weight pensioners. The only thing being removed here would be the skid marks out of their cream and brown y fronts.

"Keys please lads," Said one of the dinosaur doormen.

"What's he on about man, keys? We only had a gram to start with and we snorted that gear ages ago," mumbled Doug.

We showed our chalet keys and walked past. These doormen didn't seem to be as thorough as the ones at the other places and let us by without a second glance. There were two entrances in and out this club which were both quite steep ramps up, and landed you basically meters away from one another and you could almost taste the strong chemical vapours half way up the ramp. The main bar was huge with lots of good looking girlies behind juggling bottles and making cocktails. As I looked to my right hand side and walked over to the edge of the rails looking over the balcony two big Scottish girls lifted up their tops to show me their tits.

"Oi Oi" I shouted "Hort check this out"

Hort grabbed his Bud and slid it up and down between the fatter ones jugs, she also had two bottom teeth missing.

'You'd earn a fucking fortune at Butlins as a dentist,' I thought.'

I had to make a point of asking each girl I spoke to smile first at this rate, because coming down off the drugs was going to be bad enough, never mind waking up with a toothless Munster in my bed. Breakfast in Minehead ain't looking too good at the moment!

Both girls left showing every other fucker in the building the same as they had us as we hung over the balcony glaring at the views that you'd only expect to see on Baywatch.

"Bastard, look at that," I said, pointing towards a boob jobbed blonde prancing from out of the edge of the foam completely covered in wet fluff.

"I bet she takes it up the jotter," said Az.

"Up the arse, I'd crawl over broken glass to use her shit as toothpaste," added an exited and not so confused anymore Stana.

"Stan, I was only joking, that's a geezer."

"Fuck off mate, if that's a bloke the Pope's a smack head," he replied laughing.

"Is he?" Doug asked.

"Let's walk around the front of the dance floor so we can get a better view of the fanny," said Hort, who had disappeared within seconds.

It took us around 10 minutes to get there as every ten paces we were bumping into gangs of wet slippery party girls who were also 'off their heads' on pills.

At the front of the huge dance floor, were fifteen steps down to get to where all of the foam was laid. In each corner of the floor on scaffold built platforms, were foam cannons the size of huge dustbins with three people to each cannon to stabilize them as they shot thirty feet long gushes of the thickest foam I've ever seen before. The dance floor itself was crammed with fifteen hundred people with most of them dressed in bikinis and some in club 18 to 30's t shirts. Underneath one of the monster cannons, at the rear and to the right, stood a group of reps waving their hands in the air winding up the crowds with radio micro phones as a proper bollocks Ibiza house tune came drumming out of the sound system.

"Fucking hell bro, this is the dog's," said Az as we claimed our land at the top of the stairs and started bouncing up and down to the heavy vibes and pumping tunes. The pills we'd been scoffing all night seemed to come up tenfold. This was one of the best buzzes, all the lads together pissed, whizzed, pilled and charlied up at the same time at an Ibiza foam party. Topless fit girls absolutely everywhere and not a moody party spoiler in sight 'Heaven' wasn't a sufficient word for how we were feeling.

I looked to the bottom of the stairs where a little skinny lad about seventeen years old stood pale faced with his left hand over his mouth and sick seeping out of the gaps in his fingers as he tried to hold it back. His right hand was pulling up his boxer shorts as his ball bag dropped out of the side of them. A group of girls who were close latched on to him and covered their mouths in hysterics at the mangled mess which stood in front of them. The poor bastard couldn't hold it in any longer and released his own jet of what looked like the fish and chips that he'd eaten for dinner earlier, and then fell backwards into the foam. Two reps came walking by and I pointed the problem out to them.

You have to be a little careful at foam parties because not many people know that you can easily drown at them. All of the liquid lies on the floor and a few mouthfuls of that choke's the fuck out of you, especially if you could hardly walk properly in the first place.

The reps dashed down the stairway and started to search the floor area that we'd just seen him fall down in but he was nowhere to be seen.

'Shit' was he lying down on the floor being trampled on? I put my glass on the shelf at the edge of the balcony and jumped down the stairs in pursuit. You couldn't tell by looking where the edge of the carpeted area and the edge of the Dance floor join was because of the amount of foam that was everywhere. I lost my grip on the ground and slipped flat on my back into the heaving crowd, blinded and traveling into lots of legs and feet at some speed. I must have knocked over six or seven people before I managed to get back on my feet. Wiping my eyes clear of foam I looked around to see the flight of stairs where the rest of the lads were. 'Fuck me' I'd slid around twenty feet and could just about see enough to notice that Hort and Stana were crippled up with laughter hanging over the rail at the edge.

"Come on then, get in here you wankers," I shouted.

Az dived down the stairs too, and had managed to get where I was without making a fall.

The reps could see I had found the lad with the swinging knacker sack and they started to clean him down with bottles of mineral water. I think he was just more pissed than anything and when his friends had turned up you could see that they too had trouble keeping their eyes open.

Az moved under one of the cannons, which had just been switched on then Hort came over followed by Doug then Stana. There were two blokes dancing next to Stana and I was just behind him.

"That geezer keeps winking at you Stana. I think you're in mate"

"You better fuck off. If any ginger beers come close to me I'll be de-bagging them with a carver you cheeky bastard," he replied.

Doug locked on to the wind up and started to smirk, crouching down into the foam and pinched Stan's arse.

Stana looked directly at the two blokes and at the same time they both gave him a smile then nodded. He tried to run towards them but

Doug had grabbed hold of his leg again bowling him arse over tit into the foam. All you could see were arms and legs swinging above the foams surface in his desperate struggle to get onto his feet. Eventually, his head popped up with one arm then his whole body.

There must have been loads of dirt on the floor where he'd fell because when he stood back up without removing any of the foam he looked like a giant corneto with brown and black bits allover his head.

"Fuck sake some dirty bastards had a shit on the floor under the foam Stan," I told him.

"Yeah man, its all in your hair mate," Doug added.

"Bastard, it stinks proper bad as well," Az added.

Stan bowed his head and went into a frantic panic slapping all of the foam off his face at 100mph. There really wasn't anything there, but we were having so much fun laughing he just stormed off towards the toilets over by the smaller bar where we'd been standing earlier, and he was spitting everywhere on is way. I nearly choked myself inhaling some of the foam in an attempt to get my breath back.

Four pissed girls came over trying to cause a foam fight. One was chunky and the others looked ok. Well, from the waist up anyway. The foam cannons had stopped for the minute so the level of the foam had dropped. One of the better looking ones came over and pushed herself against me putting a big ball of foam on my nose. I put my hand under the foam and grabbed her arse. I squoze it gently and at the same time she zipped down my flies.

Ever had a girl wank you off surrounded by 1500 people at a foam party? At that, she slipped her knickers to the side and jumped on Mr. Wriggly with her legs wrapped around my back.

For the first time in my life I felt like I was being abused! One of her friends came up behind me and started to undo my shirt and knee me in the arse backwards and forwards whilst I was being ridden by her friend.

Nobody had a clue what was really going on who were around us as far as they were concerned we were fooling around. Even her friend behind me hadn't got a clue until she'd tried having a tug of Mr. wriggly herself and found out he was a little busy banging away at her faster moving friend and at that she quickly moved away stopping the strip and went to whisper to her friend 'Chunky'. I could tell what had been said because Chunky's jaw had dropped to foam level. They both bit their bottom lips which made me put a bit of a show on with the washing machine movements and all. You may as well put one on if your being watched, you never know some other foam lover may like what she sees and decide to have a go as well

'Every holes a goal' or so they say!

Shortly after, she jumped off and I packed away the stonker.

I hope to fuck there wasn't any girls in the same area later who hadn't took their pill. For all I know I could have 500 kids all born on the same day whose moms loved foam parties in Ibiza. Now that would be something to write about, wouldn't it eh? In fact, I should have missed that bit out because I could have the CSA after me for back payments of half a million quid. What a reunion that would be '**The World famous, Champagne Shane, mass conception Fuck party at Cuntlins.**' Proper!

Stana returned from the toilets looking all clean and groomed. He smiled a 'What have you been up to smile' across in my direction as he'd seen that at this point I had two not so bad looking dollies dancing one either side of me, half naked.

As I sent one of them over to him he stood as if he was about to bolt off. He obviously thought I'd told one of them to drag him back in or something. On appearing out of the bubbles with a transparent bikini on showing how fit she was Stana changed his mind and took a cool stance. The next thing you saw was the pair of them in one of those 'eat your face swap spit snogs.' I stood there and watched for a few minutes casually looking across at Doug, Az and Hort who too were standing knee deep in thick foam, arms folded and watching Stana. He looked happy, real happy. Maybe on his way to the toilets he thought, in the corner of his mind, that his night had been fucked up, basically because he looked like a giant corneto that stunk of shit. I saw a glisten reappear in his eyes. His happiness had been replenished. I still never told him to this day that she'd been blowing me off on the dance floor just seconds after I'd shagged her mate while he was in the toilets. Somehow I felt guilty and didn't want to spoil his fun. We were mates anyhow so sharing things didn't matter did it?

Sorry mate, but some of the back doorings had to be paid off! lol

We all removed ourselves off the dance floor and knocked what foam was left on our clothes off.

"Doesn't that foam taste salty Stan?" Az asked, trying to make sure Stan heard him. He didn't and we just left him to it. One of the other girls and chunky came to the bar with us and we got them a drink.

"What's your name, Kylie?" I said to the chunky one.

"No, Tina, why did you think it was Kylie?" she asked.

"Because you should be so lucky, lucky, lucky, lucky"

The smaller one punched me in the ribs and told me to stop being cheeky to her friend.

"Sorry pretty girl, what's your name then?"

"Sarah" she replied waiting for a cocky comment in return.

"What you drinking then Sarah?"

She took a step forward in relief of me not trying to take the piss out of her and whispered.

"Malibu and coke please"

"And Kylie, I mean Tina?"

Chunky smiled and took no offence. I felt sorry that she was all alone I wondered where my mate Owen Strickland was when you needed him eh? He was always normally there to bail the fat birds out.

We grabbed a bottle of Moet champagne in a bucket of ice and asked if there were any strawberries. The girl behind the counter received a twenty pounds tip compliments of Hort and went off to the cocktail bar to find us some. While she was gone the bar had been left empty so we robbed 200 Benson and three fifty pound notes from underneath the till tray. We just couldn't help it could we. They didn't have enough red coats to cope with us did they? And the only real thing we had in common here was that we were all extremely 'Hi de fucking high!'

Blondie came back behind the bar, big smiles and all and gave us a fresh bucket of strawberries. A pissed young lad reached across and tried to take one from the bucket and Az intercepted with a smack around the gob. He fucked off quickly with a fat lip.

"Blondie you've just been nominated our favorite barmaid of the night," I said, as she walked past frowning unimpressed.

Doug started fumbling around in his pockets as if he'd lost something. I'd only just realized that he'd been bouncing around in the wet foam with whatever was left of the pills in his pockets. I saw him ask Hort if he'd given them to him to keep, but Hort tapped his pockets and shook his head. Doug bent down then pulled out a plastic bag full of mushy brown stuff that resembled Weetabix.

"Oh fuck," cried Hort.

I'm not at all sure exactly how many back up pills he'd mashed, but I heard Hort saying there was at least twenty. Hort took the bag from him and we both went to the toilets to get a closer look.

We pushed open the spring loaded door and walked into a cubicle. The foam had seeped inside the bag and mashed all but six of the pills. We took those out and wrapped them in toilet paper. When the toilets became empty I smacked the button on the hand dryer and attempted to dry the mush out. It started to become hard work as every thirty seconds someone came into through the door for a piss. One of the cubicles had an 'out of order' sign on it so I took it off, put it on the outside of the main door and stood with my back to it while Hort did all the drying.

"Were going to eat this wrapped in little pieces of toilet paper," Hort said.

"Hang on, let's see if it's dry enough to snort first," I said, crushing up a small ball on top of the dryer making two quite large lines out of it. We both stood there watery eyed finding out that it was similar to snorting battery acid. On the way out we tore the sign off the door and threw it in the bin at the side of the bar.

Stan was up the bar talking the head off salty lips who had just put back on her bikini top.

The line we'd just sniffed was a little too much and my eyes started to stream tears.

"What's happened?" Stana's face turned a little concerned. "Why are you crying?"

"I've just broken one of my nails on the way out of the toilets. I can't believe it," I told him.

Sarah looked down at my hands and realizing I was pulling her leg she kicked me in the shins.

"We've just had to dry all of that shit out in the toilets," Hort, had gone all fidgety and kept looking around nervously. Shortly after, he leant against the bar and threw up all over the red patterned carpet.

"You ok mate?" frowned Az.

"That was a fucking bad idea snorting all of that shit Shane," he said, as his stomach contracted a second time.

"I don't feel too fresh myself to be honest," I told him, as I passed the water to him and leant up the bar myself.

He swigged back half the small bottle, gargled, and spat it out over the floor next to the circle of pizza looking spew.

"Fucking hell Doug, we nearly lost all of that gear then mate," Hort told him goggle eyed.

"We're gonna have to just bomb it in paper now, but not to worry it hasn't lost any power, Hort and I have just snorted a dry line in the toilets and believe me, it knocked the bollocks out of us," My nose had started to run, so, putting a finger on the opposite nostril, I sniffed an almighty sniff. I nearly choked and felt as if I'd snorted sand and cement. I wouldn't be doing that again in a hurry.

The majority of the clubs were coming to the end of their tether. People were knocking over tables of glasses, being escorted out, puking up the walls and on the floors. I'd seen at least three throw up in the foam as we'd moved over to the balcony rails again, closer to where the reps were standing, to give us a better view of the crowds this time. We'd spotted two lads appearing from the foam plastered in the sick that must have been lying on the floor as they fell over. Lovely feeling, knowing you've been lying in a pool of nice warm puke and humming of it for the rest of the night. 'Mmm tasty carrots!"

She wrote her number down on my left arm with a felt pen she'd borrowed from one of the reps. It would have been nice to have go with her, but if I got it so easy by the end of the night she'd have probably of had more cock than Joan Collins (sorry Joan) so better to grab something a little fresher I thought. I didn't like the idea of shagging a tin of chicken soup to be honest. Crude I know, but true nevertheless.

My watch read 2:15am which I reckoned must have been the time that I'd gone arse over tit in the foam because the second hand had stopped and the inside of the watch looked like a spirit level.

"What's the time Hort?" I said, then noticing he wasn't next to me anymore and that he'd also took it upon himself to bounce up and down on one of the reps on the dance floor. I looked at my other options. Az didn't have a watch. Doug was nowhere to be seen and Stana was doing his captain caveman dance near the balcony.

There was a table a few metres away with six lads standing around it. I tried to walk towards them in a straight line, but my legs had turned to jelly. Eventually I managed to get close enough to speak with one of them. Two of them looked at me and the rest carried on dancing around the table. I'd forgotten why I'd gone over in the first place and looked at the floor, racking my brain for a few seconds.

"You ok there mate?" one of the younger ones asked.

"Yeah mate safe. I'm completely off my bollocks and was going to ask you something but for the fuck of it, I can't remember what it was."

Nudging his friend and frowning he asked me exactly how many pills I'd taken. I tried to count on my fingers but gave up after four and just shrugged my shoulders.

"Fuck knows mate, six, seven, Charlie, skunk, whizz, Jack Daniels, vodka, champagne, stuck a bottle up a girls fanny, two blow jobs and a shag in the foam. Shaking my hand and buzzing of what I had told them they invited me to stay for a while, or at least until I could remember what the fuck it was I wanted in the first place.

I later found out it was 3:30am and was having so much of a good time that I'd forgotten that all the lads were probably wondering where the fuck I'd gone.

"Listen lad's, I'll see you in Hurricane Harrys later ok? I've got to find the rest of the crew I came with, ok?"

I don't think any of them heard or understood a word I'd said, but they shook my hand and away I went. I hate it when this happens, you're high as a kite your legs, eyes and head are all 'game over' and you're trying to find four other people who are in the same state, if not worse, amongst two thousand people covered in fucking foam. I paced up and down. Down and up. Everyone's faces didn't even look like faces anymore. It was really weird because I was sure I'd passed myself at least twice. 'Where the fuck are they?' Maybe they'd been looking around for me and thought I'd fucked off or something?

I kicked open the double doors and held on to the rail as I carefully attempted to walk down what seemed to be an extremely steep ramp to outside. There was one of the pensioner doormen standing in the way of the exit. I could feel him staring at me as my head was bowed. I looked up at him with the expression of a psycho serial killer and he moved to the side. As much as I wanted to say 'cheers mate good night' I couldn't. I felt like I had a grip on a high voltage pylon and couldn't let go.

As soon as I reached the fresh air the only thing I was good for was sitting on the wall by the side of the fairground rides, taking in deep breaths.

Lots of people were walking back and forth past me, screaming and singing in drunken stupors. Two girls and a boy at the side of Barnum's were trying to hold up another girl who was completely pissed out of her head. Her legs had completely stopped working and gone to jelly. Her head had flopped back with jaw swinging and mouth wide open. She looked more or less asleep all but for her groans. The boy had both his arms underneath her armpits while the girls were lifting her legs as they pulled her along. The problem was the girl must have been 4 feet 11 tall, weighed 15 stone and the face on her looked like Nora Batty's brown un!

The boy stumbled backwards a few inches and fatty slumped back on her arse. All she had on was a big red and white 18 to 30's t shirt and a shitty yellow pair of bikini bottoms with loads of clock springs sticking out at the sides. My stomach churned at the sight as three more boys passed by cheering with a group of girls who all had their hands in the air. You could see that one of the girls had broken the heel off her shoe as she walked along like Bob Marley, shivering in the cool night air.

Over at the side of Barnum's the 18 to 30 monster was still there stuck on her arse outside the front doors. No one could pick her up because she was too mashed. Peeling myself from off the wall, I walked back inside the club to try to get the doormen to go and help. I couldn't go near her she looked scary.

"Excuse me mate."

"Yes sir, how can I help you?"

"Well, it's not me that needs the help believe it or not. There's a dirty yellow Volkswagen beetle outside collapsed on the floor with a broken clock under the bonnet. All its friends have been trying to jack her up for a while, but they don't seem to be able to do much, could you take a look at her to see if you can help?" I asked.

"What, someone's parked a vehicle outside?" the one side of the doorman's face lifted higher than the other, "Where's the car again."

"She's outside to the left of the main entrance," I added, walking back outdoors and pointing towards the group of people who were now just standing around the girl trying to decide the best way to get her up.

The doorman walked over and caught a 'full frontal' of what I was on about. He eventually managed to drag her over to the nearest wall which she was able to lean her back up against. He got a small bottle of water from inside and gave it to her friends, instructing them to try to get her to drink it in attempt to sober her up a little. As he walked back towards the door he lifted his left hand to say thank you for bringing it to my attention.

"What about the broken clock?" I shouted, as he shook his head then smiled.

"Definitely not a Rolex is it that one?" I added.

After thinking about it I spewed over some dodgy looking plants over the wall. You always feel much better after being sick for some strange reason it sort of gets your head back together doesn't it? I decided to take a piss close to the fire exit and kept myself standing up by resting my forehead against the wall.

Doing a quick helicopter I put Mr. Wriggly away and went on a hunt to find the others.

I took a left turn at the archway and walked along for 200 metres. The bridge and moat, which we'd seen earlier at Harrys, was lit up in green with lots of spot lights surrounding the ridge of the roof. It didn't look that busy from the outside and all I could see was a couple standing on the bridge pointing into the water below and the side of a doorman at the front entrance on his walkie talkie.

Approaching him I tided myself up and tried to put on one of those I've not necked loads of drugs and booze faces on, which was some fucking task I tell you. Walking across the wooden bridge I nearly tripped up because of the uneven stature of the boards.

"Can I see your key sir?"

I showed him my key and walked passed. I was going to ask him if he'd seen the lads come in here earlier, but decided not to, it would have come out all wrong. My brain knew what I wanted to say, but I was sure my mouth wouldn't have so I gave it a miss.

There was a tunnel which led to the entrance of the club which also was lit up by green and yellow spot lights and the ceilings and walls looked like they'd been molded from fiberglass. The colours it had been painted and the reflection of the lights gave the effect that you were walking into a cave. It looked well impressive. As I reached the bottom of the tunnel, the floor stopped ramping down and became level again. This place had been well designed. The whole of the inside looked like an underground cavern, again all molded from fiberglass, Sprayed green, brown and yellow. To my direct left was a waist high double rail and a green pool with various coloured fishes swimming around inside. As I walked further around there were two food kiosks selling burgers, chips and pizzas. 'No thanks,' food was definitely not on my agenda and would have been going straight back down the toilets if I smelt it for another second. There was a small dance floor for around 200 people down a flight of six steps with a river type theme running alongside. On the right of this was a narrow carpeted area and then a much bigger dance floor with a tall sectioned off DJ console more or less in the middle of the club. Behind that was a very small circular bar. The main bar stood at the bottom of the venue and ran across the full length of the back wall. Scattered all around the interior were high standing tables and chairs. At this point it looked like there were 800 people inside, it was quite Smokey and visibility was low.

'Ok lets grab a drink and scout about' I said to myself. After a 15 minute stand up the bar I eventually got served then, instead of giving me JD which is what I asked for, they gave me JB which I fucking hate by the way. Another 5 minutes later and a little explaining I'd got what I wanted and was sitting at a table smoking a Marlboro light. They had to be in here somewhere. All the things we'd planned had been made clear that this was where our final stop would be. A tall blonde girl walked passed and pointed at one of the chairs on my table. I smiled, and gave her the sign that it was free. Wishful thinking that was. I thought she wanted to sit down, but she just took the chair and fucked off with it, 'Fucking lesbians!'

I picked up my half full drink and walked around the edge of the big floor trying to catch glimpses of the people's faces through the thick cherry flavored smoke, which was being pumped from machines above me.

Nothing, I didn't even recognize a single face, not even from the other bars either. I swigged back the rest of my drink and walked past the DJ console. Something caught my eye. There was a tallish bloke hugging a life size plastic tree next to the small bar. The closer I got the more I could see who it was.

"Fucking hell Hort, what's up with you? You ain't gone all 'green' on me have you son?"

"Ooooh, I feel all funny Shane."

Hort was not looking good. He looked pale, distressed, dripping with sweat and seemed a little worried.

"Where are Doug, Az, and Stana?" I thought. Have they joined Greenpeace as well??

"Fuck knows. They're in here, somewhere. I feel really ill I do," he went on to tell me and we decided to go outside to get him some cold air.

We grabbed a bottle of cold water and both walked up the cave tunnel to the front doors again. After crossing the wooden bridge we found a brick wall and sat down.

Every so often you can throw a 'funny one' especially on E's if you take too many and go on a paranoia trip. You can convince yourself that everything is 'on top' and go all insecure about nothing. It's not a nice feeling at all and can completely ruin your night if you let it. The best remedy is a bit of fresh air and a talking to which pulls you out of it.

I explained what had happened in Barnum's earlier when I'd lost the plot and forgot who I came here with and he told me that they thought I was with a bird somewhere and decided to meet up later.

"So what sort of a state is Doug in then?" I couldn't even imagine.

Hort rubbed his forehead "He was throwing bottles at everyone by the archways and nearly got us into a big fight. Then he tried to open up one of the fair rides with Az and we all were chased off by the camp security. I'm well surprised we got in here." Hort replied, livening up a bit.

"And Stana?"

"Stana just keeps moving around from person to person talking them to death and I haven't seen Az for about an hour,"

It must have been getting really late because there were hoards of people pilling out of the bars and clubs and collecting near to the arches. Bottles were being smashed to the ground and the screams and shouts of the paralytic party goers filled the once quiet skies with life again.

"Shall I build a spliff to bring you down a bit Hort?"

"I don't know about that Shane, I'll just start tripping again as soon as I even smell it."

"I'll just put a little bit in then Hort ok?"

We both stood up and took a few paces to the side of Harry's. Hort stood there nodding his head to the beat of the bass that could be heard from the fire exit doors, while I built a tidy looking reefer.

"Look at that Robert. A fine looking spliff if I ever saw one"

"It smells a bit strong to me Shane. You said you were putting a bit in."

"I did put a bit in," I told him, "A bit of weed, a bit of pill dust and a little bit of coke which I'd stashed away earlier."

A few tokes on that worked wonders. It smelt like we were smoking old socks and flip flops, but other than that she was a blinder! After a we had a couple of drags each I put it out because the trees had all started wilting and I thought we would benefit from a little mind bending later.

The front security waved us passed this time remembering our faces (what a sight they must have been) As soon as we touched the level ground I spotted Stana leaning up the burger stall."

"Oi Oi," I shouted .Stan pointed towards us and as we got closer he shook my hand. He'd obviously been explaining to in detail to the dolly behind the counter about his long lost brother, because she too gave me a look and smile as if to say 'where the fuck have you been?' The club had become packed out with large gangs of St Trinian's dancing on the tables which were supposed to have been for the diners. I could now also recognize lots more people from the 'foam party' who were now slumped up the walls and rails chatting away, swinging their feet to the beat of the music, the majority with Smirnoff bottles in their hands.

"Is Karen in here do you know?" I asked the burger stall girl.

"From the Irish bar you mean?"

"Yeah, that's the one. She told me that she'd meet me here after work"

"Are you the one who gave her the pill?"

"Me? I haven't given anyone a pill, why did you say that?"

"Oh, nothing," she replied.

The burger girl pointed over to the centre of the Smoky club and told me that was where she'd last been seen dancing.

"Come on Stan lets go and nose about." Hort said, spinning around

"I'll be over in a minute."

The burger girl smiled and must have been happy with the company so we left them and walked towards the dance floor.

I turned around and pointed at the counter "Make sure you put plenty of salt on his chips darling,"

"G'on Stana, show her your sausage." Hort couldn't help but to join in the fun.

For the first time in four hours I caught my first glimpse of Doug. He was sitting on the edge of a high chair close to where the lesbian had robbed my seat an hour or so ago. His head was pointing toward the carpet he was nodding slightly and he kept putting his hand to his mouth every so often. Hort and I decided that he needed a bit of attention and took him a bottle of water over and as we approached him saw that he was still munching pills. "Where the fuck did you get them from Doug?" Hort didn't seem impressed.

He looked us both straight in the face then returned to the position he'd started in.

"Come on Doug sort it out," Hort put his hand on Doug's shoulder and shook him hard.

"Eh?" Doug could hardly make a noise.

"Where did you get that bag from? Fuck me look at the state of you!" Hort shouted in his ear.

"It's me sandwiches man, me sandwiches."

"Doug, first you waffle on about cakes chasing you and now you're eating a bag of sandwiches? Come on mate, get a grip." I tried to act quite serious, but it was a struggle as I had a flashback of the jam donut standing on the door in the Irish bar again.

"What sort of sandwiches are you eating then Doug? Let's have a look." I said, as I took the bag from his hand and saw Big fat yellow things with a Mitsubishi imprint in the middle.

"I got 'em off a geezer who works here. They're alright man, honest."

"Fuck me Doug, if you thought these were your sandwiches mate you must have made a very big mistake mate!" I pointed out. Doug looked up with concern. "They look to me more like Mc Donald's Bacon double fucking' Cheeseburgers with mayo, red sauce and everything else you could chuck on the fuckers. Nice one Doug." I added. As a huge pill grin appeared on his face knowing he'd just done something right.

I ate one straight away and Hort did the same not long after.

Doug had told me that he'd already taken six or seven and that he'd only bought them half an hour ago. If what he told me was true, the next two hours were going to be the biggest roller coast rush ride ever.

It takes around twenty minutes for an 'E' to 'Come up'. If he ate six the first one should be kicking in about now, then every ten minuets the rush should double until he's got the full 'six pack' rumbling his nut to bits! We tried to get him to walk around with us, but he insisted that his legs wouldn't allow him to.

"We're going to find Az then Doug ok? Are you sure you'll be alright?" I hated leaving him, but I was 'Off it' as well and so there he stayed in zombie mode.

Az was nowhere to be seen at the moment and we'd got our hands full with the drunken girls who had changed from 'prim and proper' and now after the amount of piss they'd drank, were arse and ball bag grabbers.

We took the opportunity to snog as many as we could, but on my drug fuelled lust to go on a Butlins 'snogathon' I ended up slobbering with some messed up rep who had just been sick in the toilets. She held my head from the back and pulled it towards hers as if we were meant to be Siamese twins. I felt a piece of something go inside of my mouth and a horrible acidic pukey taste which coated her tongue went inside with it. For the fuck of it I couldn't pull her away .I felt suffocated and struggled to gasp for air. Both of my hands pushed her away from the shoulders and as I did this I too vomited a jet of sick all over her face and down the front of the 18 to 30's t shirt she had on.

"Errrrrr, you dirty fucking bastard," she screamed, looking down at the multi colored puke I'd just passed her for free. All of her friends were horrified at the mishap, Hort was on his hands and knees in hysterics and when one of her mates had seen him she launched a drink over his shirt. He then grabbed two from off the table and drowned the girl I'd just jet washed. Her mates caught him throwing more booze and he tried to pretend that he was washing her down. Things started to get out of proportion at this point, and I thought a fight may have broken out quite soon. From out of nowhere a hand appeared and pulled me from the middle of the crowd.

"Az, where you been bro?" I was shaking my head at this point still thinking about what that girls tongue tasted like.

"I've Just been wondering around off my head," he told me.

We pulled Hort away from the now red faced angry reps and decided to make a sharp exit from the bar area. Fuck knows why they'd started getting arsy with us, anyone even with a cast iron stomach would have reacted the same as I did if some smelly puke bitch had just spat the 'carrots of truth' into their mouth. The only thing I was pissed off about was that the Mitsubishi I'd just popped had been vaulted up at the rotten bastard too.

I had to get to the toilets to clean the front of my top down which I decided to take off to wash completely. Just before we reached the toilet doors an arm pushed out in front of us. "You can't walk around here with your top off mate; you'll have to put it back on"

"I'm walking into the toilets behind you to wash it then it'll be straight back on," I told him.

He went on to tell me if I didn't put it back on I'd be escorted off the premises.

"Alright, he's just told you it's going to be washed." Az started to get pissed off with his attitude.

The security looked straight in front of him and didn't reply. If I'd have slapped him across the face he would have probably started crying, the prick. He looked as if he'd been more at home on the door of Marks and Spencer's. We walked passed him and pushed open the door.

The toilets were flooded and smelt like Steptoe's Y fronts. There were five sinks with smashed mirrors in front of them, but at least one of the soap dispensers had a little soap left inside. I gave my top a good wash and rinsed it out properly. All of the hand dryers were fucked so I rang it out as much as I could and put it back on wet, but not smelling of bitch sick anymore.

A young lad came bundling in from the door and fell flat on his back, sliding along with his hands on the piss flooded floor. Fuck knows what he was going to do about the smell on his clothes. He had a pair of white jeans on and a blue shirt which was hanging out. We helped him up trying not to touch any part of him that had been swimming.

"Where did you think you were then kidda, the water park?" I said, amused that not only I had had a few miss haps tonight.

The kid didn't know what to say. He turned around and all the back of his white jeans that had probably been brought just for the holiday had turned black, brown and yellow. The shirt he wore had dripping cuffs and the bottom part at the back was soaked. We left him to it. We'd got enough of our own problems trying to get a grip on reality and pulled the door open to go out.

The Marks and Sparks retard had changed his position to right outside the men's toilets. I don't dispute for one second that it was to make sure we'd all got our tops on. He looked disappointed to see we were all clothed correctly and gave us a look of disgust as we passed him.

"Errrrrr, mate there's a lad having a shit on the floor in the cubicles," Hort said.

He pushed open the door and popped his head around. We just wanted to annoy the miserable cunt for being such a sour faced twat. His face on return told me that we'd half done the job.

Back inside Stan had stopped chatting to the fast food girl and found Doug, who at this point was making growling noises like a lion with a bad tooth.

"Take those pills off him Hort, he's gonna end up 'brown bread' else."

Hort took the bag and put them in his pocket. We got Doug off the chair and on to his feet. At first he stumbled a little then steadied himself on a barrel table with both hands. Don't forget at this time we were 'all' completely mangled, except Doug was a little worse. I grabbed both sides of his face and looked into his eyes. His left one looked up towards the ceiling and the right one down to the floor then they started moving around in circles as bloodshot as eyes could be.

"Let's get him outside Shane." Hort, wasn't feeling too fresh either, but made a point of trying to help nevertheless.

We dashed what was left on the table and lifted under Doug's arms in an attempt to get him outside. Stan and I waved to the burger girl as we departed and made our way through the long tunnel to the exit. Doug weighed a ton, and it seemed to take ages carrying him out.

Eventually, we saw the bridge, crossed it, and plonked him down close to the arches.

"Deep breaths Doug, deep breaths you greedy fucker," we told him, as he looked like he was going to cry at one stage. With his face changing so many times it was pretty difficult to latch on to his true feelings.

"Pass me two of those Mitsubishis Hort. In fact, give me four."

"You can't do a four drop Shane you'll be worse than Doug is."

"Let's have a little two drop each then. All of us."

"I ain't having any more yet," Stan seemed a little put off at the state of Doug, which was understandable I suppose.

"Come on Stana, part timing as usual?" Az didn't need any encouraging as he bombed two straight down the hatch.

I have never needed my arm twisting to do any drop, but always had to charm others to follow suit.

"Let's see if the supermarkets still open to get some drinks." I said, but noticing that the shutters had been pulled down we gave it a miss. After a little fucking around sorting Doug out, we all agreed that it was about time we tried to find the chalet.

Now, we had between us five key rings with five different chalet numbers on and none of us after our mad night out could remember which the one for our gaff was.

"Fifteen, blue brick," Doug whispered.

"Shut up Doug, fucking blue brick. None of the keys mention blue bricks."

"Didn't one of them have a wood in them?" Az asked.

"Mine says 'bear wood'," Stan said

"And mine says Edward," replied Hort

"I'm sure I would," I added as two soaked girlies passed me by.

All went silent for a moment as we all followed the girls with our big eyes.

"Redwood, that's it, Redwood," I remembered that Doug was the holder of the original key.

We decided that the best route would have been past the Irish bar, as this was where we had started the party. We walked down the centre of the archway passing the shoe shop, fish and chip shop, supermarket and at the bottom we strolled passed the Irish bar where Mr. Kipling's security had stood outside hours before and the heroin Woolies inside.

"Right," I said. "I think we need to walk straight down towards the log cabins, and then it's somewhere on the right." I wasn't sure at all where that would take us, but it just came out and sounded convincing enough.

"Are you sure Shane?" Hort didn't seem too convinced.

"Trust me lads, its down the bottom end of the complex remember it took us twenty minutes to get to the first bar?" I hoped so anyway.

"I think you're right bro, it is at the bottom half," Az nodded in agreement, pointing in front.

Now the lighting situation on the complex was far from Blackpool illuminations. In fact the little street style lamps which were placed either side of the main pathways looked to me as if they'd been switched on to economy mode . If any old grannies had been out sleep walking or wife and husband swapping in the middle of the night there was going to be some major casualties in the morning because I'd got the biggest pupils on the complex and I could barely see a fucking thing.

We walked for around ten minutes, but not a log cabin in sight.

"Are you sure there are log cabins down here? I can't see anything but chalets with names that I've never heard of," Stana had started to doubt me, but none of us had a clue so we all kept on looking.

"Don't worry," I told him "It's further down there. Just keep walking."

We heard music in the distance which sounded as if it was coming from our right hand side.

"Listen lads, party," Hort was gone before he finished his sentence.

If he thinks something's going on without him, he won't stop until the party is surrounding him. I chased closely behind. We couldn't see any chalet lights on, but as we ran through the rows we banged on everyone's doors in case they'd accidentally fell asleep early.

"Its coming from down there Shane," Hort pointed at three blocks of chalets. We could see a glimmer of light coming from the window of one of them, but when we got there it was the wrong place and the music seemed to be coming from the next block.

"Come on Shane lets go in."

"Hort there's no fucking party in there, someone's just left the light on that's all."

He pushed the door and discovered it was unlocked, then went inside.

'Fuck that' I told myself 'it looks like were robbing the place.'

In a few seconds I was expecting a big heap of shit going to hit the fan.

"Where's Hort bro?" Az turned up behind me.

"He just broke into that chalet with the downstairs light on. He's been in there a few minutes now," I told him, as we both pushed our ears to the window to see if we could hear anything going on inside. There seemed to be a few people talking inside, but no commotion. I couldn't work it out.

"What's he up to?" Az couldn't work it out either.

We waited a few more moments and moved backwards to the facing chalets so we could have made out we were having a piss if any one passed.

"Maybe there is a party Az, shall we knock the door and see?"

Just as I spoke the window closed and the light went off.

"Something's wrong here mate .He couldn't of gone in, pulled a bird and gone straight to bed in under 3 minutes."

"Well if that's true, he just smashed my record from when I used to work at Bushwackers. Fair play to him!" as I spoke the chalet door creaked open and Hort appeared not with a bird or a black eye, but with four massive cheese and union sandwiches, on crusty bread. Az and I just stood there, gob smacked, speechless, and frozen to the spot.

"Please tell me I'm tripping Az, or has Hort broken into that chalet, made some cheese and onion sarnies in the kitchen, waited until everyone went to bed and then crept out through the front door?"

"Couldn't of put it better myself Champers," Az nodded.

"Hort," I said quietly, "who's in there?"

"D'no, I walked into the living room where there were four or five people having a drink and asked them if they minded me grabbing a drink from the kitchen. They said 'yes help yourself,' so I made some sarnies, pissed in the fridge and left through the other kitchen door," he told us, pulling a bag of crisps from his trouser pocket. Hort looked quite chuffed.

I looked at Az and shook my head in amazement at what I'd just been told. In fact it amazed me to the extent that the half spliff that I'd saved from earlier became lit again quickly.

"Here, get some of that in yer bloodstream."

"Fuck knows what you've put in here Champers, some kind of paint stripper I take it by the burning sensation in my chest."

"Its all good stuff," I told him, "No worries."

Doug and Stana caught up with us. "What's going on here? We wondered what you were up to." Stan said, seeming to be much livelier than ten minutes ago.

I couldn't explain what had happened with Hort because the flip flop spliff had crossed too many wires in my head for me to be able to speak anything else, but complete bollocks.

"Why's Hort got crisps and sandwiches man?" Doug had popped out of his coma for a one off question.

Az explained the best he could and Doug farted at the excitement he'd just downloaded.

"Fuck me Doug, turn it in, that stinks proper......"

"Like a rat died up your arse," Az added, finishing off the sentence for me.

"Who was that bloke you were chatting up in Harry's Doug? The blonde headed one?" I said on the wind up.

"What bloke man. Fuck off,"

"You saw him didn't you Az?"

"Oh yeah, the one with the leather studded cap you mean?"

I nodded my head and pointed at Az. "Yeah, that's the one, with the leather cowboy trousers on with the arse cut out of them,"

Stana put his hand on Doug's shoulder which was quickly pushed off "Fucking hell Doug, I'd keep off the drugs if I were you mate,"

"Listen man, you can all suck my dick," Doug frowned.

"I think we touched a nerve lads what d' you reckon?"

"Leave me alone, my head's already fucked up without the sad jokes from you lot."

We walked in search of the party, but seemed to get further and further away from the sounds. Hort turned around. "This is near to our chalet, look at the cabins over there," he pointed out.

He was right, I recognised the log cabins wed passed on our way out, and a big sign saying Redwood.

I jumped up in the air "We're here lads," I felt like Harrison Ford in 'Raiders of the lost Ark' for a second. I don't know why, but Flip flop spliffs can be hideously mind altering.

We opened the door of the trashed accommodation and sat down on the bed and chairs. Compared to the outside it seemed quite hot in there. Hort was still munching on his stolen goods and Doug was still all fidgety and switched on the television. The dance music of earlier had changed to some mad 'It's me I'm Cathy' withering heights shit.

"That music's doing my nut in Stan. Put something else on bro, you just have to press the button on the top right corner of the remote," I said, and as I spoke some very strange things started to happen.

I was sitting opposite Hort and I drifted off for a few seconds with my eyes closed. When I opened them, I could see that every time I breathed there was a jet of thick white smoke coming from my mouth which was exploding into stars and shit like a firework display.

"Hort look at that," I said, blowing towards him.

"Look at what Shane. What you looking at?"

I explained what I was seeing then blew out.

"Fuck me, I can do it as well, watch," Horts face had seriously freaked out as he'd started tripping of what I'd told him, and now he too was able to do it.

Stana's face wore a deep frown for a while as he watched Hort and I blowing in the air at each other and then bouncing in our seats at the fire work type explosions only we could see.

"I can't believe it," he said," Shane and Hort have completely lost it! I've been telling them for ages if they kept on taking so many pills and other shit, they'd eventually end up mental. Look at 'em both, blowing at each other. I've never seen anything like it in my life," he added shaking his head.

Doug started giggling, rocking backwards and forwards on his chair and pushing downwards on the edges of the wooden seat nearly lifting him off it.

"It's Shane's famous flip flop spliffs combined with mad trippy pills. A lethal concoction," Az confirmed, shaking his finger from side to side.

"I really don't care, Hort do you?"

"Hello, Champers calling Hort can you hear me? Come in Hort."

He seemed too busy looking above me to respond. "Az, look at Shane, there's something wrong with Shane,"

Az looked at me, trying to work out what he was going on about. "I can't see anything Hort,"

"There are sparks flying out of his head look, look!" he screeched. jumping up off his chair he darted into the bathroom.

Have you ever tried to prevent something, but couldn't think fast enough to do so? Hort bowled out of the bathroom. He'd filled the long pot which holds the toilet brush with water from the bathroom, and in the best interests of saving his good old mates head from melting, launched it at me. As he did, it somehow span and twatted me on the side of the head, drowning me with germs that Domestos wouldn't kill!

"Cheers Hort, I was just about to ask you if there was any 'toxic waste' around in the chalet for me to drink"

I had just been contaminated with the DNA of the past 25 years of happy campers and quickly started to strip before I blew up into a big purple balloon. Hort stood there and, realising it wasn't real what he'd seen, apologised. "I could have sworn you were on fire Shane honestly!"

"Ok Hort, well you certainly put the fire out anyway. We were tripping mate, don't worry about it," I said

I decided to take a shower and replace my clothes with something that seemed less attractive to the flies that had started to gather around me.

"Shall we go back out and rob some of the boats off the camp?" Doug said enthusiastically.

"They're on a lake you mad cunt. Where you gonna paddle with 'em, round and round in circles?"

"Shane's got a point there Doug," said Az "You'll probably get caught trying to do a runner with those you know. We could go swimming though instead?"

"I'll give that one a miss; I'm just drying myself down after Horts Anthrax attack." I informed them.

Az got up and put on his jacket. "Come on, let's go out then. We'll leave Champers to stay and warm himself up a bit, if that's what he wants."

It was light when they left. Doug followed them at the back like a stray dog as they went out to find the lake and boats.

I turned over the TV and some early breakfast cartoons came on. Putting my hands under the mattress I found the bud of marijuana which had been put by as back up. Jim's girlfriend 'Lotty' always used to 'stash' buds away in secret places so that when we thought there was nothing left, it was a blessing to see we'd got 'back up smoke' and we smiled like the Bee Gees we did.(I was well stoned when I wrote that!)

After a little fumbling around, I made something that looked half smokable, and sparked it up.

The chalet had started to get hot and a mist appeared across the windows where the water from the bathroom had started to evaporate. I rubbed the window behind the pinkish curtain and peered outside for a second. There wasn't a sole to be seen but for a few sparrows eating the crusts of bread that Hort had thrown away. I unplugged my mobile from the charger and pressed hard on the button. It lit up a bright colour white, which blurred my vision for a second before my eyes adjusted to it. A few seconds later it beeped to inform me I'd just received three text messages. I could hardly stand never mind read and lay there with the phone still in my hand thinking about some of the things we'd done last night, and then it dawned on me.

'Shit, the Spice Girls.' I thought, as I sat up straight. I looked at my phones screen; it read 7:13am.

I had a rough idea of whereabouts I'd left them, but it was light now and very possible that the camp workers were wondering around and they may have seen them. I had to go and get them, just to see the lads' faces when they'd returned coz none of them had got a clue what I was on about when I'd tried to explain it in Barnum's earlier.

Peeling myself off the bed, I had to sit still for a short while, as my head had started spinning. Az had left one of his coats, so I put it on and went to the bathroom to see if I looked like 'Kiss' but without the makeup. I had a yellowish tinge and looked fucked if I tell the truth, but fucked or not fucked, the Spice Birds were mine and that's what I had to do.

As the front door opened, the chill of the morning air hit my face and felt nice and fresh. The birds who'd been eating Horts left over's had all fucked off. They'd probably all be dead by 10 am if Hort had left any of his DNA on the sarnies. Either that or they were flying to Mars or something mad. I took a left turn at the end of the row of chalets and started to walk on to one of the main pathways towards the archways again. I don't know why, but it seemed much colder as I walked on passed the dining hall. As I glanced to my left I could see the caravan where they were hiding underneath and quickly looked around in all directions to make sure no one was watching me.

Just to the side of the archway was a shopping trolley. The sort you get at Asda or Sainsbury's. I pushed it by the side of the caravan and took another look around. Still 'all clear.' I bent down and put my head more or less underneath the van and grabbed Scary's legs. As I pulled her from underneath I looked up and had a terrible shock. The caravan's curtains had been pulled to the side and all I could see was an old man and woman in their late seventies staring down at me, with quite concerned looks on their faces. They popped open the top window.

"Mornin'," I said, trying to think of a way out of what I could be getting into. "I'm the camp maintenance supervisor, sorry if I've woken you up, but I noticed a little rubbish underneath your caravan and thought it would be better off in one of our site bins," I told them.

"Ooh, right," said the old lady .The way old ladies do.

"What exactly is under there?" questioned the old man.

"Nothing to be alarmed about. Just some old advertising boards and stuff. Better to move it out of your way. You don't want rats in your caravan do you sir?"

"Rats, what do you mean rats?" the old fellow had started to play 'head movies' about being eaten In the middle of the night.

I was digging myself a grave here. Why the fuck did I start ranting on about rats. "Nothing to worry about sir, we here at Butlins pride ourselves on holding the award for the cleanest camp in Britain. I was only referring to some other less modern camps that you knowingly seemed to avoid."

They both smiled and nodded. Fuck knows where all that bollocks came from, but it did sound convincing, even to me. I breathed a sigh of relief as they both waved and the curtain was redrawn.

I put Scary in the trolley and bent down to get the rest of the mob.

"There you go love."

I banged the back of my head on the sharp edge of the caravan with the surprise.

"I've made you a nice hot cup of tea."

I can't believe it; I'm robbing the Spice girls from underneath someone's caravan on a camp site I'm not even supposed to be on, absolutely off my tits tripping. All my mates have gone to steal the boats off a lake somewhere else on the site and this old dear is trying to keep me with a cup of tea. Paranoia kicked in full pelt.

"Oh thank you but I've got an upset stomach and can't drink anything for 48 hours. I would have loved that tea as well. Maybe another time," I said, loading the rest of the girls into the trolley.

"Oh dear, my Bill's had the 'runs' since he's been here," she said with her hand on the side of her face. "You don't think it's the water do you?" she whispered.

"No love, get him on the baked beans and eggs he'll be shitting logs again in the morning, trust me."

What the fuck was I saying? 'Shitting logs???'

The old dear stood with the caravan door open and gave me a little wave as I pushed the trolley away. I ran as fast as I could and when I got to the chalet heard a shout from not too far away. Hiding the trolley around the corner I managed to smuggle the girls in and close the door. I placed them all standing at the bottom of the bed and hung up Az's coat on the back of the door. 'That was proper mission impossible material 'I said to myself. "What do you reckon birds?" I jumped onto the bed and sparked up the other half of the spliff I'd left in the ashtray.

The girls all seemed to stare at me. Well they would do I suppose, wouldn't they, that's how they take the photos innit. Stupid!

I stood on the bed with a shoe close to my mouth. "Right then girls, tonight is your lucky night. I understand that you can't sing for me so I'm going to sing for you. Are you ready?'

"Now… here's a story from A to Zee,

You wanna get with me you've got to pop a fuckin' 'E'.

We've got Stan who's the man lives in a caravan.

We got Az on the raz who gives it all he has.

We got…."

The front door opened.

Stana just stood there with the most frightful, unusual expression that you could ever imagine. Doug appeared at the side of him and then Hort.

"Fucking hell, Champagne Shane's got the chalet full of women man, and we've only been gone an hour." Doug looked amazed.

"Where did you meet these Shane?" Hort said pushing through the door, picking up scary and starting to do the waltz with her.

Stan and Az were a little curious how I'd managed to get them into the chalet in such a short time. Eventually I drummed it into everyone what had happened. Well, at least I thought I had anyway.

Doug was standing at the bottom of the bed and every time he thought there was no one watching him I could see him trying to whisper in Ginger spice's ear.

"What's going on here Doug, eh?" I said, "You ain't trying to nick my birds are you?"

He sat up straight. "Nah man, nah."

We all pretended to carry on talking to each other and ignore him. Again he put his head close to the cardboard cutout. "Ignore them all man. Ignore them. They're all mad," he said, returning back to his position quickly.

"What was that Doug? Did you say something then?" I asked him, with a raised eyebrow.

Doug's eyes were moving shiftily from side to side. 'For fuck sake man, you're paranoid you are,"

I pointed to the bathroom door "Oh, so you won't mind if a take Ginger fanny to the shower for a shag then, eh?"

As I spoke I walked towards the edge of the bed where Doug was now standing and he jumped up and stood in front of the cardboard cut outs. "Come on lads leave it out. I've been with 'em all night, I've promised to buy all of their Cd's and look after them and that." He then looked at the floor, trying to work out why he was trying to protect five cardboard cut outs from his friends.

"Doug, in the first tune the Spice Girls recorded they sang. 'If you wanna be my lover, we want to share with your friends. Don't you remember?"

He turned his back. Mumbled something to Ginger, nodded his head and turned back around. "They said that they're not like that anymore. It was just a song and they don't want to share with anyone."

"Oh, is that right. Which one of them told you that then Doug?"

Doug scratched his head "Ginger."

Trying my best not to laugh I stood up and closed the door. "Well, why is it that every time you face us, all five of them stick their fingers up and bob their tongues out behind your back, so that you can't see them, eh?"

He blinked a few times and started to move slowly to the left. What I'd told him had sunk in as I could see he was making an eager attempt to catch them out. His head moved around quickly and he pointed at them all with a humorous 'Ahh, I nearly caught you' type of face.

Hort and I broke into rib cracking laughter. Stan and Az covered their mouths on the bed unable to contain themselves.

The tears were streaming down my face. "Doug, take a look at Ginger and baby spice's arse and tell me what you think."

Staring at us with extreme caution incase it was a trick to steal his girls. He walked around to the right of them and looked down at Gingers arse.

Doug's face turned a claret colour realizing he had been body guarding five cardboard cut outs." It's all brown," he said. "I think I'd better not take any more of those things," he quickly added.

'Bump! Bump! Bump!' The door received a not so friendly Butlins knock.

I looked around at Az and whispered. "Turn the music down bro I think it's the camp security."

I had to hide the Spice girls, but trying to put them under the bed wasn't happening. I took all of them into the bathroom and left the door ajar so I was able to hear what was being said. Everyone was still moving stuff around quickly as if we were on a TV game show against the clock. Pushing it under blankets, under the bed, sitting on stuff and finally, trying to act casual, which was probably our biggest task of all. Az opened the front door. "Good morning lads, I'm sorry about the music being so loud, but the button on the remote had stuck, we resolved the problem and there's nothing else to worry about."

I could just about catch a glimpse through the door, noticing that the two camp security who were in there late fifties were sporting fat beer bellies and were both as bald as coots. The one closest took a step forward "Would you mind if we took a quick look in your accommodation please sir?" he said pushing the door, which in turn Az signaled for me to lock the bathroom.

Az frowned "Well first I want to know what it is you're looking for. You are looking for something right?"

The guy at the back nodded "Yes. Some of the site advertising boards have gone missing and you seem to be the only people awake on the complex making a noise."

"We want just quick peek inside, that's all. Then we'll be on our way," added his friend.

Az opened the door and pointed in towards the main room. Doug and Hort pretended to be asleep while Stana sat on the chair trying to be interested in whatever was on the TV.

One of them put his hand on the bathroom door. "And in here?"

Az tutted. "Are you still in the shower Shane?"

"Yes, hang on mate" I said, as I quickly stripped off all my clothes and turned the shower on full blast with me and all of the Spice girls inside.

The man popped his head around the door as I jumped out of the cubicle. The bathroom at this point was full with steam and I walked straight to the door looking pretty pissed off. "For fucks sake mate, ain't you got anything better to do than bother people at this hour of the morning?"

He gave me a short wave. "Sorry mate. Please accept our apologies." And then he pulled the door to.

All the girls had big grins on their faces, but I suppose they would really, being in the shower with a superstar like me, 'Lucky fuckers.'

All the towels on the floor soaked and surrounded by puddles. I dried myself with one of the bed sheets that was in the bottom of the wardrobe and walked back into the living room. "Listen lads, were going to get in some serious shit here soon after the thing at the lake as well you know."

Stana told me that they had robbed two paddle boats from the boat house and had some other security running around the lake trying to capture them. Doug reckoned that we needed to be getting off the site today or they'd be calling the 'old bill'

Az picked the keys up off the table." We can't be going anywhere yet. Who's going to drive the car?"

He had a point. I was having trouble controlling the Asda trolley earlier never mind smoke a turbo charged Porsche full of lunatics on a come down up the motorway.

Stan stood up. "Let's grab all of our clothes, stash them in the car and if it goes arse up we can at least get off the camp without leaving anything behind. They won't have logged the car coming through would they?"

We collected all of our belongings, dripping clothes and all while Stana located the car and began to load it up.

Hort started unscrewing the TV. "We'll soon flog this Shane and get a few cerveza's with the money."

"Turn it in Hort. I can see us getting lynched for aggravated burglary and kidnapping the way we're going." Az said.

Hort dropped the knife he was unscrewing it with and grabbed his bag.

We made our way towards the main pathway.

Stana returned with an asthma attack after loading up the motor. "There's a lot of commotion going on near to reception. I may be a little paranoid, but I reckon it's about us lot." He said, still gasping for air.

"Let's go and grab some breakfast and decide what to do with food inside us then," Hort said.

I agreed, at least if we got a tug we could say sorry and explain that we didn't hurt anyone or damage anything and that would be that, sort of.

The thought of food made me feel quite Ill, but we always made a point of eating something after a binge. You have to re-fuel the fire as we always said.

"I could manage a cup of tea and toast," Az said.

"Yeah, me too," said Hort. Stan agreed, as we approached the dining hall looking around to see if anyone had followed us.

"Are you feeling any better Doug?" I asked, raising my eyebrows as I smiled.

His head was pointed downwards. "Yeah man. Fucking hell, that was a mad night man. Proper,"

We sat down in the big Butlins diner and blagged a breakfast with the stolen chalet keys we'd acquired. Doug took a bite of his bacon sandwich, chewed it three times, spat it back on the plate and filled his mouth full of egg.

I looked across the table at him. "The eggs are 'off' man. I've just chewed a baby birds head, Errrrrr."

Doug fucked off to the toilet having already swallowed a mouthful, which I must admit tasted quite nice. I just can't help winding people up me. A few uniformed guards walked past the glass paneled diner. One of them glanced in, but didn't really seem to be after anyone in particular. I headed across to the toilets to check on Doug. The last but one cubicle was closed so I walked down and kicked the door. "Fuck me Doug, you stink."

The sound of Doug pebble dashing echoed through the toilet. "Ooooh bastard, I've got the trots a bad un, man."

"Hurry up mate. We've nearly finished our 'embryo' on toast."

I heard a gush hit the toilet door and a pool of yellowy brown liquid dropped to the floor.

"I'm going to get a cup of tea and I'll bring you some water, okay Doug?"

"Mmmmm," was all I got out of him as I gave my hands a quick wash and pushed open the swinging door to get back to the table.

Az was busy talking to one of the servery girls, asking if it was possible to buy some more Jack Daniels.

"Sorry, it's only just coming up to 9am. You could try the super market, but again, I'm quite sure they too aren't allowed to sell booze until after twelve o clock." She told him.

Another waitress came and stood behind her. "I think the

supermarkets closed today. Something went on last night and this morning one of the supervisors was unable to get a newspaper. He was ranting on about health and safety or something."

As 'off it' as I still was, I knew there was no way that Health and Safety were closing the supermarket because I'd kidnapped the spice girls from outside. Ok, so we'd left an off license full of empty bottles behind the fridge, but I'd worked in enough wine bars and clubs to know that the bottles alone wouldn't have done it. They'd more than likely been removed and that would have been that. I decided I was being totally paranoid and put the thoughts to the back of my head.

Four girls came strolling in and sat down in the far corner of the diner. One of the waitresses smiled at them and walked over.

The toilet door swung open and a slightly pale Doug appeared looking a touch 'off his nut'. "I hope that pan was insured, because I've just written it off!"

"It didn't smell too fresh when I left you mate so fuck knows what it smells like now." I told him.

Doug staggered closer to our table. "It's the first shit I've had since we left..." He stopped in mid sentence as the waitress returned with the drinks and went a funny purple color.

"Tea?"

"Yes love and the water's for this young man here," I said pointing at Doug.

Doug grinned. "Listen to Shane spinning the bollocks on the women."

I stood up at the table and pointed at Doug who was now cowering like a dog at what I might say. "This gentleman here, has just shit up all of the walls, and puked up the door in the cubicle of your nice clean toilets. He may be young, free and single, but he's a dirty cunt as well you know!" I added.

She looked me straight in the eyes and with a face like thunder stormed off towards her friend, who had just taken food to the girls in the corner.

All six of them looked over and a few of them giggled.

I shrugged my shoulders. "See Doug, I was just being polite and you have to go and spoil it making out I was on the pull again."

"Did you see the face on her when you told her about the toilets?" said Az, "I think she fancies herself a little bit anyway that one"

I finished off my tea and pushed the cup forwards. "Well if they fancy themselves a touch, a bit of rough and ready sorts them out every time."

"G'on you slags," Hort said, waving his tongue out to them, as if he was about to exercise a 'muff diving' attack.

Hort and I considered staying for another night and decided that we could have got dressed in the swimming baths. Everyone else disagreed, especially Doug. "I think it's a bit moody y' know."

"Why Doug," I asked, "We haven't really done fuck all if you think about it. I bet there are loads more things gone on last night without our antics mate."

One of the four girls stood up and on her way to the toilets and passed by our table.

"Hey, sugar lips," I shouted, as she looked around and pointed my way. It was Karen from the Irish bar.

She walked over. "Hello stranger." Her eyes were quite large looking.

I smiled, pleased to see her "You still buzzing off that round thing?"

"Yeah big time, I haven't been to bed yet."

"Neither have us lot. We're just waiting for the off license to open so we can get some more booze, but 'snooty tits' over there told us that it'd been closed down."

She nodded "Yeah, there was a big problem at the super market early this morning. Something about food I think. I don't really remember I'm still off my cake on that pill you gave me.

"Quite strong aren't they? We ate about fifty between us last night," I told her.

"Honestly? You looked bad in the Irish bar last night. I tried to find you in Harry's. Jane, the burger girl told me you'd been asking for me, but it was too busy and Smokey to find anyone in there."

"Bad wasn't the word," I said, "It was fucking mad."

"I've got to be at work for twelve. I'd better go and get some sleep," she told me, walking off to the toilets and waving.

Doug was all fidgety and paranoid again. "Let's get out of here man, come on we've got to go." as he stood up adjusting his coat.

'Grumpy tits' came over and apologized, telling me she didn't know I was a friend of Karen's

"Don't worry darling I was just having a laugh with you that's all," I informed her.

She gave me a peck on the cheek. "Sorry I bit your head off. I haven't had much sleep myself."

Az tapped his pocket. "We've got something here that'll liven you up."

"That's why I haven't had any sleep in the first place." She said, as he passed her one of the Mitsubishi's Doug had mistaken for his sandwiches.

It brought a smile to her grumpy face.

"Bacon and tomato flavor those ones," I said, and she walked away trying to work out what the fuck we were talking about.

"So right then, what're we going to do. Stay, or chicken out? No ones robbed any boats because they're still on the lake. If they do tug us for them we can just pay for an hour's rental. What can they say? I'll go and grab 'Ginger fanny' and the crew then hand them in at the supermarket. I may even get a reward. Then we're safe again," I told them.

Stana didn't look too convinced and Doug, every time I mentioned staying turned white, but Hort half agreed.

"Hort listen, I think you're forgetting something. You do realize that we've officially paid for today as well.

Az raised his eyebrows. "Fuck me, I'd forgotten about that."

I left them to chat in the diner and went on a mission to return the Spice girls, hoping that I didn't see anyone who'd spotted me kidnapping them earlier. This time around I carried them over my head occasionally dropping them because they were still wet from taking a shower with me, "lucky Fuckers'. I reached the arches, walked through and plonked them all down near to the shoe shop.

The supermarket shutters were three quarters pulled up and I could see three people emptying the remainder of the fridges at the rear with another two mopping up.

"Excuse me." I said in my politest voice.

One of the assistants came over. "I'm sorry but we're closed mate."

"I've just returned the Spice girls. They were by the side of a caravan around the corner and I remembered that they were outside the shop yesterday. I think someone may have moved them just for a joke." I explained.

"Oh, right. We were wondering where they'd gone to. Thank you very much sir."

I smiled. "My pleasure. Would it be possible for me to by some drinks?"

"We'll be opening later sir. We've been busy emptying the fridges all morning, but when that's done it'll be open."

Karen turned up behind me, chatted with the assistant as I began to walk away called me. She explained to me what had happened and had found out why the place had been closed for the morning. She found it quite funny, but if she'd have known what I knew, things would have been a little different.

I ran away with my hand on the top of my head, not believing what I'd just heard. Wait until I relay the info to the lads back at the diner.

"You're not going to believe this." I told them, as everyone sat up in their seat with the change of tone. "This morning, someone bought food from the fridge at the supermarket, took one bite out of it, then collapsed on the floor and died. I think it was one of the camp security." I added nervously.

Doug went white, started shaking, and then fucked off to the toilets again.

"What's up with him?" Stan queried.

A quarter of an hour later he returned with bad bloodshot eyes. "Come on lads let's get the fuck out of here man."

I stood up. "Yeah, let's go back to the chalet then."

Doug scratched his nose. "I want to go home man. Like right now!"

We headed towards the chalet and just as I put my head around the corner spotted three or four people hanging around outside our place with another standing in the doorway. I turned back around quickly. "Shit, they're raiding our gaff."

If the truth be known it was probably room service tidying or something, but the majority of us we're full blown paranoid, especially Doug who started to slide off. "Listen, we need to be fucking off right now. Do you get me?"

We all followed him towards the car park, but no one could understand why he'd freaked out so badly until we were driving through the exit gate.

"Doug, why have you got a blanket over your head, we're off the complex now?" asked Az.

He still wouldn't let on what his problem was, so I helped him along a little. I nudged Hort and nodded towards Doug.

"Loads of police buzzing about ain't there Hort?"

"There is a few. I wonder what's happened."

"Well," I said, "according to what Karen had told me, 'Old George' the longest serving security guard at Butlins had gone to work early this morning and popped to the supermarket to buy his usual 'favorite breakfast' to eat with his hot flask of tea." I paused for a minute and glanced to my left where Doug was pretending to look out of the window with a very, very pale face. I winked at Az.

"What did he eat to kill him bro?" Az asked.

I sat up and arched my back. "Well, Karen reckoned it was a cake of some kind."

At this point we had just pulled up at a set of traffic lights and everyone in the car looked around at me in confusion, well, all except Doug that is. I nodded my head towards him and smirked to let everyone know I was on the wind up. "They said that someone had been tampering with the fresh cream éclairs inside the shop."

Stana seemed quite bewildered. "How do you mean tampering?" he asked, pulling away from the lights as they hit green.

"Apparently they've got someone on the C.C.T.V in the super market crouching over an empty cake carton having a shit. He then sprayed fresh cream from the can either side and put it back in the fridge! Along came 'old George', grabbed his éclair, sat outside pouring himself a brew and took a big bite and swallowed it. They reckon they'll match the DNA and photo and have the cunt behind bars before the end of tomorrow for murder."

Doug flipped his lid "Let me out the car man, stop, stop the car." He screamed as he jumped out and darted off into the bushes where he threw up something that resembled an after birth.

We were all streaming tears inside while Poor Doug thought that he'd killed someone. We tried to tell him we were fucking him around, but he was having none of it. It took us a while to get him back in the car and eventually we set off once again.

Old George had 100% gone to pick up his morning treat, but when he opened the lid at the till he could smell shit. The camp manager had called the food supplier and closed the shop for the morning while the stock was removed from the fridges. I could remember Doug was ranting on about cakes chasing him along with the plastic carton he'd appeared with and I put two and two together.

No matter how much I tried to reassure him I was joking he wouldn't believe me and ducked down in the back of the motor every time someone mentioned the word 'Police'.

A few days later, there was a news flash on the radio claiming that some holiday makers had complained that they had seen groups of people in Butlins, Minehead 'out of their minds' on drugs. Some of the camp workers had been arrested and charges were being made.

George, I heard, had gone off his 15 year long habit of scoffing chocolate éclairs in the morning and settled for good ol' tea and toast. As for the Spice girls being kidnapped, nothing was ever mentioned, but for sure, old Bill on his beans and egg diet would have now, definitely been shitting logs once again. I never did get any thanks for that!

We returned to Butlins a few more weekends that year, but could never seem to match our very first visit. Doug used to switch his mobile off if he even suspected we were going to ask him to accompany us.

Still to this day, he wakes up in the middle of the night in a cold sweat from the constant nightmares of being chased by chocolate éclairs!

The Aldridge Girls

WHY ARE WE WAITING

I've been locked up in Tenerife II penitentiary now for 16 months. My lawyer Alfonzo Delgado appealed against our case going to Madrid for falsification of currency, because there was no false money! The prosecution suspended the case from being sent until the machinery and computer which had been found at the hotel had been analysed. The report came back four weeks ago and then it took them another three months to come to the following conclusion

'The machine, which has been analysed from case number 3058/2003, along with the portable computer 'with adequate software,' would have been able to read and rewrite the magnetic bands of credit cards. For this reason, we recommend that this case be sent to the Audiencia National in Madrid for a charge of falsification of currency, fraud and international organied crime.

On four occasions I have applied for bail on medical grounds. I have suffered a severe loss of sight and at present am blind in my left eye and have lost 70% in my right. Along with the appeal I have entered six reports from different hospitals both Spanish and British to confirm that since November the 4th 2002 when I was involved in a huge gang fight in Tenerife I had lost my visibility and was waiting to go to court for this case, where I was the victim. I have on various occasions tried to contact the British blind association for help whilst I have been here via the British consul in Santa Cruz and 'Prisoners abroad' (A small charity to help British nationals who have been locked up in foreign jails.)

The British blind association said that because I was at present in the Canary Islands they were unable to help me and the Spanish blind association said they can't do anything because I was British!

My lawyer on various occasions has asked the prosecution to give the reason for me being held on remand and what it is exactly there saying I've done in this case for them to be refusing my bail applications.

The lawyer informed me that the court stated that I'm being treated in the prison sufficiently and that the only reason I'm here on remand is because I know the others. No one said I did anything. No one has accused me or seen me using a credit card or even pointed me out in an ID parade. It's basically an empty accusation! The police had found one dodgy credit card and a matching passport which was completely legal. The person whose name was on the card admitted that it was his, and told the police that he'd paid 3000 Euros for it. In the Royal suite, where two of us were staying, the police 'apparently' found various types of drugs, a laptop, a few video cameras, which were legit, and a large white machine which was a magnetic stripe reader/writer. Every hotel in the world has one of these to program the key cards which allow you to get into the hotel room. This is what they found and are trying to give us a possible 20 year sentence for. One credit card and a machine you can buy legally in fucking Tandy's.

Rene Jansen, the Dutchman was freed some months ago for supposedly transporting 5000 pills onto the island. On trial day the court informed him that the witnesses hadn't turned up and by the time they'd been summoned, his max four years on remand would have expired.

Danny O'Connell was in court in Jan 2004 on a murder charge. He too had been on remand 3 long years. His lawyer on trial day had advised him to accept the 10 year sentence the judge was offering 'or it may go to twelve' she explained, advising him to take it. He sat there for a short while and decided not to accept. Twenty minutes later in the courts cells his sentence arrived early.

They gave him a 1 year sentence and he walked out free that same day without a word mentioned about the two years too many that he'd spent waiting, surrounded by the incredible head games and torture of the primitive system which we're in as I compile these memoirs.

This week, an Italian man was taken to court in Tenerife for currency forgery and fraud. The amount which had been forged was 700 Euros or five hundred pounds. The judge and prosecutor were asking 13 years each for him and his girlfriend. He will receive his sentence in around three weeks he was told. Over here you never get told your sentence in the courts like in England, instead, some three euro an hour Spanish screw hands you a piece of paper telling you that you've just got a ten stretch. If you want to appeal it's necessary to do so within a period of 3 days. Get your heads around that one!

TENERIFE UNCOVERED

It was freezing cold and pissing down with rain. Our plane left Heathrow airport at 10.30 pm. We'd only just reached junction 12 of the M6 and it was 8.45pm

Elvis was glaring out of the window at the storm. "Fucking hell Orange peel, put your foot down!"

"I'm doing 120 mph the car won't go any faster!" He bit back.

I switched my phone on. "Chill out, we'll get there in time."

Hort was already at Manchester airport with Nobby, checked in and necking vodkas as fast as they could to start off the holiday in the airport bar. I'd never been to Tenerife before, but Hort had given it his stamp of approval so I thought I'd give it a try. We were unable to get the flights from the same airports so we had to split up and fly from two different ones.

Elvis had told his missus that he was off to the Isle of Man to change his driver's license and would only be gone for a few days. She would have told him to 'fuck right off' if the truth would have been told. My mobile rang.

"Hello, is that you Shane," Hort shouted over the airport tannoy.

I pushed the phone close to my ear "Hello Robert, what's happening"

"Are you nearly there yet?" he asked.

"No, are we fuck. Were still miles away Hort, and the plane leaves in about an hour or so."

Horts phone made a crackling noise as it tried to grab better coverage. "Don't miss the plane for god's sake. I'll have no-one to go on a bender with else."

"Hort, we're going flat out. Elvis is having panic attacks in the back about the time already!" My phone beeped three times and then cut out.

Elvis saw me look at the dead phone, took it off me, and put it on charge in the rear cigarette lighter.

I didn't see another car pass me for the next 45 minutes. Our little red Astra was screaming out for another gear and the rev counter was brinking the 'red line' Elvis appeared between the two front chairs" How much longer you reckon we got to go Neil?"

"Not that much I don't think, we should start seeing signs any moment," he replied.

After another 20 minutes we saw our first sign.

'HEATHROW AIRPORT, 30 MILES.'

"Aren't we supposed to check in an hour before take off?"

"Yes orange peel, but if they hold us to it we'll probably be fucked." I told him.

Eventually we got there, parked up and made a dash to the Airtours desk. They'd closed up.

"Excuse me darling," I said, to a smart looking middle aged lady who turned around and came to the desk. "Hi, can I help you at all," she said in her best stewardess voice.

I showed her our tickets and explained that we had traffic troubles on our way. I touched the spot where the Airtours contact number was printed on the booking form. "I called the Airtours office telling them that we were going to be ten minutes late maximum and they informed us that someone would be here to book us in," I explained.

She tapped her pen on the point of her nose. "Oh, they did leave a little early." She politely allowed me to use the phone at her desk to connect to Airtours head office where I explained what had happened to us.

"I'm sorry sir, but although the plane is still on the runway, regulations won't allow you to board at such late notice."

I gritted my teeth. "Listen, your representatives left early. We've been here since an hour before takeoff and the fuckers at the desk haven't. It's yourselves that are at fault. We complied with regulations. Now take down this mobile number and tell me when our next flight is or you're going to have three very unhappy customers growling at the next staff that turns up at your desk OK!"

"Ok sir, give me ten minutes and I'll call you back with an alternative."

Neil sat on the floor with his back to the wall and his chin resting on his knees. When stood up he was a staggering six feet seven inches tall. "I can't fuckin' believe this. What we gonna do now sweaty?"

Elvis shrugged his shoulders.

"Don't worry," I told them, "they'll have to book us in on the next flight out free of charge."

What a start to a holiday. I'd just tried to bribe the airport security to allow us on the plane with a fake Gucci watch and a fifty pound note, but he was having none of it. "I'm really sorry, it's beyond my control," he told me.

We eventually got to see someone in person at 9.30am the next morning. He told us that there were no more flights available today, but tomorrow morning at 6.30am we could jump on a flight to Tenerife via Gran Canaria.

Elvis banged his hand hard on the desk and big Neil moved forward "We've already spent hundred and fifty quid in the airport last night because of this you twat!"

"We need compensation," Neil added.

We ended up getting free passes to eat at Mc Donald's and Pizza Hut and around twenty hours more to wait.

I rubbed my stomach. "I can't eat any more food. I wished they of give us a pass for a 'free for the all' off license eh? Tight cunts."

Slightly bored I scanned the huge diner area which was surrounding us and noticed they operated a 'none waiter/waitress service' for the food outlets. I sat there for a while with my head resting on my hand and elbow on my knee. A couple of metres away I spotted a table with three Mc Donald's hats on top. I got up and walked over.

Neil lifted his head. "What you up to?"

I cleaned the rubbish from off the table and emptied the ashtray. Then put away the food trays and binned the leftovers. Elvis and Neil were watching like two dogs would a square of chocolate.

"Watch this." I told them, as a family of four was searching for a table.

"Good morning. There's a freshly cleaned table just here to seat four persons. Sit yourselves down and I'll collect your orders for you," I said with my 'happy hat' on.

All four of them smiled. "Thank you very much," said the lady as I sat the two children down.

"Right then, what would you like to order? Don't tell me, 'Happy meals,' with chocolate or strawberry milkshakes for the kiddies? I said, as both kids bounced up and down on their chairs in agreement.

"Yes that's fine," said the man, "the wife and I shall go for the ... Big Mac meals."

"Excellent" I replied.

I walked over to the counter, ordered the meals and gave the brunette behind the counter my pass.

"Right then, that's two happy meals with strawberry milkshakes for the kiddies and Big Macs, with fries and cokes for you."

The lady handed me fifteen pounds. The bill came to twelve and she told me to keep the change.

"Thank you very much sweetheart. I hope you enjoy your holiday," I said with a big gleaming Ronald Mc Donald smile.

Neil and Elvis had to turn their backs to laugh.

We sat there for the best part of three hours and I raked in a tidy wage being an undercover waiter.

I finally sat down. "Right then, I've got about three hundred quid here. lets fuck off to the bar I need a drink."

We traveled up the escalator and walked in the lounge. "Three quadruple Jack Daniels and cokes and six Diamond whites please darling," I told the barmaid, who was now looking around for the rest of the people she'd thought I was with.

Elvis took a step back. "Calm down Shane. We'll end up missing this plane as well."

"Nah Elvis, this is a well deserved drink. I've been working as a waiter for the past few hours and its thirsty work mate I tell you."

"You're completely off your head you are," Neil grinned, seeing what I had concocted out of nothing earlier.

We downed the first one which rendered big Neil watery eyed.

Elvis started looking around. "Not much 'grumble and grunt' in here is there. Are you sure this isn't a gay bar," he said nodding over towards a gang of biggish looking lads.

"They look like rugga players sweaty," Neil pointed out.

"For fucks sake let's not go over there then, I've got a bit of history of rowing with rugby players," And I explained to them about the 'Woolies' at Butlins.

A few hours later everything seemed much better. Well, I suppose it would do wouldn't it, as there wasn't much blood left in our alcohol systems at this point. I thought it would be a good idea to call Hort to see if he was having better luck than we were. His phone went straight to answer machine so I tried again and all I got was "fuckin' hell" and the line went dead again. Something didn't stack up and I couldn't understand why he sounded so moody.

I went to the public telephone and called directory enquires for Manchester airports flight information. They told me that the flight had been delayed, which explained why Hort sounded so pissed off.

"Could you put me through to reception please, I need to contact my brother."

"Certainly sir, hold the line."

The line beeped "Reception, how may I help you?"

"Hello, my brother is somewhere in your airport and I need to contact him, it's an emergency," I told her his name and the line went quiet.

I could hear the loud echoing tannoy through the earpiece. "Robert Horton, please come to the reception desk p. Robert Horton, to reception."

I could just imagine what he looked like staggering drunk and panicking over what the reception wanted with him.

The line made a clunk. "Ello…ello, who the fuck is it?" An extremely slurred sounding Hort answered.

"Hort its Shane what's going on? I can't get hold of you and they've told me your planes been delayed, Hort, can you hear me, Hort?"

"Fuck me Shane you had me shitting bricks then. I thought I was gonna get nicked or something. They've just called our plane for boarding I've got to go, take offs in ten minutes," and at that the line went dead.

Bars in airports should be open 24 hrs if you ask me. I mean what's the fucking point in starting off your holiday with a closed bar eh? You wait all year save, save, save or rob, rob, rob, whichever applies to you. Put your new fancy clothes on, toddle off to the airport, wallet in hand all ready to spend. SORRY BAR CLOSED. Who the fuck wants to see that then eh?

We walked around 'half cut' after a few more bevies's to see if we could find some 'airport pussy'. No chance, not even with beer goggles on. The place seemed empty and most of the flights had already gone early this morning.

Eventually five thirty came and we checked in.

"You shall be boarding within the hour gentlemen. So make sure you're at gate 23 when you're called ok. Have a good holiday," she added.

We trudged towards the double electric doors which swung open as we got closer and slowly made our way to gate 23. Some short time later they called us and peeling ourselves from the amusement arcade we boarded.

A loud beeping noise woke me up as the captain informed us that we were approaching Tenerife south airport. I glanced to the left, where my head had been resting during my sleepy flight and saw that I'd dribbled over the girl's coat that had been lucky enough to draw a seat next to mine. I quickly threw my blanket on top of the mark and rubbed it with my elbow as I pretended to yawn. The girl gave me a half 'I'm not amused' look and carried on staring out of the window. I'd probably, no, definitely snored all the way through the four hour flight as Neil later confirmed.

We collected our baggage and started to make our way to the taxi rank which was packed with confused holiday makers trying to speak 'Spanglish' to the taxi drivers in order to get to their hotels.

"Walk to the front and push in Neil," said Elvis.

Neil marched forwards. "Alright our kid, how much to Island heights?"

The taxi driver understood Island Heights and not another word of his broad Black Country accent. Neil looked around and informed us that he'd already picked up the lingo.

Elvis laughed. "He's Spanish you cunt and you just spoke to him in English!"

After twenty five minutes drive we arrived at our destination and weighed the driver in 5000 pesetas.

"Adios our kid," I shouted as he drove away.

It was around 12 midday and brinking 40 degrees. The cases were opened and shorts and t-shirt were at the ready and off we went to where Hort was staying.

"Is Hort here?" I said, to one of the girls at door number 26 Windsor Park.

"Who?" she asked

"Hort, he got here last night."

"Oh, err yeah, just a minute," she said, as the door swung open and a rough looking bird stood in front of me rubbing her eyes.

I frowned. "Just got in have you love?"

She nodded pointed into the apartment and pulled the bedroom door behind her. The gaff looked like a bomb had hit it, Pots, pans, bottles and clothes everywhere. I looked down the five steps towards the living area and saw a tell tale sign. It was just peeping out from the edge of the sofa, pale and lifeless. Horts big toe!

"OH ROBERTO!" I sang, as I tickled it with a wooden spoon that I'd just peeled out of a saucepan of food from off the floor.

As my head popped around the side of the sofa I caught my first glance of what sort of night he had. He was lying on top of an inflatable with a pair of Bermuda shorts on. His face was as white as a bottle of milk and the sweat was pouring from his forehead.

I stood by the side of him as one of his eyes opened "You ok Hort?"

"Fuck me Shane, there's some good gear over here."

It didn't seem to matter that he looked like he'd got thirty minutes to live, what seemed to override it all was that Tenerife held some serious kit. A smile appeared on my face knowing that the MDMA was up to spec.

Nobby appeared from the bathroom. "Alright lads?"

He told us that Hort had disappeared halfway through the night and he'd taken a taxi back to the apartment to get some sleep. That sounded about right I thought, as I'd too fell victim to the vanishing more than once. He was like a UFO with a bag of pills and bugle in his pocket. One second he's hovering around with everyone staring and the next second he's gone, never to be seen again. That's Hort!

The hot hot sun went down and things started to cool a little.

Nobby was nearly ready. "Right then lads, what time are we going out then?"

"It's pointless going out too early Nob, everybody starts moving around twelve," Hort replied walking into the bathroom.

We decided to get ready for nine and have something to eat first then mooch about later. Hort and I had brought the loudest shirts you could ever imagine. His had oranges all over it and mine was the fluorescent colours of the rainbow.

It was close to ten when we finally managed to get moving. The hill we had to walk down was more designed for skiers than tourists and we could have easily slid down on lino quicker. Hort's apartment door was wide open. One of the girls had just walked out of the shower with a g string on. Ripples of fat hung off her arse and right in the center of her left cheek was a huge boil which looked more like a tit.

I walked in through the door. "Jesus, some poor cunts gonna wake up with that in the morning."

"Go on Shane have a tickle," Hort said, trying to egg me on.

"Yer having a laugh Hort, I wouldn't shag her with yours you cheeky bastard."

A girl's voice shouted out of the bedroom. "You pair better fuck off or you'll have nowhere to stay tonight." She obviously was mistaking my voice for Nobbys.

"Yes lads, it's not very nice bad mouthing the ladies. They've been good enough to help you out with a bed for the night so come on, have a bit of respect." I said.

"Bollocks, I haven't said fuck all!" Nobby shouted to her.

We strolled past the water park and down a different steep hill the other side of the motorway bridge was where we found somewhere to eat at the famous 'Aberdeen steak house'. There were loads of them in the South of Tenerife which were always full and cheap as chips.

"Five pints of larger and five steak and chips with all the trimmings, Por favor," I said.

Neil rubbed his left temple. "How can they do 8oz steak with all the trimmings for 2.50?"

"It's fuckin horse meat kid, that's why," Hort told him.

"I've eaten horse before and it ain't that bad. In fact I've tasted worse pussy, I must say," I added.

Neil spat some of his beer out over the table. "I'd rather eat horse than some of the pussy I've seen you with on a Saturday night."

"You cheeky cunt, I've spotted you on a Monday fucking dinner time with some right smelly old boots, never mind Saturday nights!"

The food was eaten and the beer started to flow. More and more people swarmed the streets in search of fun and frolics. We walked down another hill heading towards Las Veronicas. This was a strip of bars and clubs on a road which lay back from the main street.

"Alright lads," said a PR girl touting for customers, "you out for a drink?"

"Do sharks shit in the sea," replied Hort.

The girl smiled. "Come in to the Crows Nest, we've got happy hour at the minute, two for the price of one and a free knock back."

We followed her across the pathway and up to a flight of stairs. The block of bars was falling apart and had cement bags abandoned at the side of the concrete steps and all.

Five minutes later we were back on the strip. The place we'd just been in was empty and stunk of piss.

"It was busier than this last night Shane. I don't know what's going on tonight. Let's try up here." Hort pointed to a few more places that were more or less the same as the first ones until eventually we got to the 'Wai ki ki bar' which was full of people on a JMC airlines pub crawl.

Tenerife felt good. The people were full of smiles and looked as if they hadn't got a care in the world. Everyone enjoyed themselves and were unjudged in their drunken stupors. I could definitely get to like this place I thought.

The week we had was fast and crazy. Pills more pills, more and more pills. Mercedes, windmills, tango oranges, double Mitsubishis. It got to the stage were Hort and Nobby were mixing a tea spoon of 'base whizz' with orange juice before leaving the apartment just to stay awake. Snort coke, smoke coke, and more coke. Fuck me things were getting out of hand.

After two days without sleep the body tries to repair and re charge itself whilst your awake. As a result hallucinations are rife. We'd probably had four very light hours sleep in six days. The pills started not to work, but we still took them, just in case. Then, we started accusing each other of not taking the pills or 'I've had more than you' and get into bitchy little arguments over nothing.

On the sixth day I went on a really bad Para trip in a club. I went back to the apartment to get a huge carving knife. I then pulled it out in the club and explained to Hort that if the people wanted to cause any more shit I'd carve them up like Sunday roast. I stood by one of the pillars in the club waiting for it to 'go off'. It didn't, but I was having none of it and slid out back onto the streets wired on loads of speed and very paranoid. They started to walk away near to the entrance of the beach at the bottom of the road near to the Kentucky. I figured that if I took them out off the streets 'like on the beach' I would be less vulnerable to prying eyes which would enable me to slip away into the dark night.

I waited about 30 seconds after the people had disappeared into the dark beach front then made my way after them. I was shaking like a bastard. Not sure whether it was the adrenalin or the coke, pill, whizz shakes I was experiencing? Standing just inside the entrance and looking around for them I looked on as they were walking along the Atlantic shore line. The beach was really quiet and I reckoned that I could have it out with them and be back at the club in a short while without being noticed.

Someone shouted something. It was probably nothing, but convinced I'd been sprung and the six lads knew I was about to 'have it off' with them I flew into a fit of rage. "Come on then you fucking bastards," I screamed as the huge carving knife sparkled when I pulled it into view. I started running towards them. They were now looking my way, wondering whether they could be in trouble or was it just some drunkard who'd gone off his nut because he'd been woken up. They saw the carver and were off. The more I saw them run the more enraged I became. They seemed to break up and scatter behind some chained down pedelos near to a rocky area. I dropped to my knees with my body ridged, staring around for them. Now were they hiding and waiting for me?" I thought, as the concoction of drugs kicked in.

I need to get off the beach and back to the hotel. What about if they'd told the police about the psycho stabber chasing them on the beach with the big eyes and runny nose? 'This is bad' I thought, now the whole of Spain are after me for attacking six people on the beach. I bet some of them were undercover coppers on a job and they'd reported me for acting weird before I done them all in? This is really really bad.'

I ran and ran as fast as I could, trying my best not to go down busy streets. I was a little confused which direction to travel in and eventually plucked up enough courage to grab a taxi.

Handing the driver a pocket full of change and saying "Gracias" I pushed his car door to as if I was diffusing a bomb with extreme caution. The room lights were off. I could have sworn I'd left one on? Maybe they were waiting inside. The police, I thought.

No, the apartment was just as we'd left it. Suitcases sitting on the floor half open, Bottle's of water still on top of the table. I was ok for now until I worked out my best plan of action. I heard footsteps.

'Bump bump bump.'

"Shane, it's Nobby open up."

I was expecting terrible news. "Are you alone Nob?"

"Yeah, what's up with you?" he'd immediately clocked on to the look on my face.

"Fuckin hell mate, you ain't gonna believe this." I told him as he walked in quickly.

I popped my head around the door to make sure he hadn't been followed, and then pushed it closed and twisted the lock.

"Right mate, we got ourselves a situation. I've just 'jibbed' a load of geezers up on the beach and theirs old bill everywhere. I need to get the fuck out of here or I'm fucked for definite."

Nobbys mind went blank. "Www, Wha, what?" he stood there for a few seconds with beads of sweat appearing on his forehead like in an advert for car wax polish. "Shane, what are you saying man? Tell me exactly what happened." Nobby turned very pale and looked drained as I started telling him my version of what had gone on. He wiped the sweat from his forehead, still wide eyed and with a heart rate of 200 beats per minute he stuck his head under the cold tap in search of a reality check.

"Nob, the reception is holding my passport and I need to get it back fast."

"But how?" he replied.

A lump appeared in my throat as I tried to swallow. Nobby gave me one of those 'that's impossible' looks as he placed his hand on top of the wooden chair in front of him and crossed his legs.

I rested against the work top next to the fridge. "You could get it easy Nob. Think about it."

The confused look on his face seemed to intensify. "But, how Shane? and why me, and not us?"

"Well," I said. "We both know that the security guard has been looking at you all holiday."

"You wanna fuck off man, Fuck right off," Nobby screamed on the defensive.

"Listen mate, you don't have to 'do' anything with him, of course not, but a little egging on would probably do the trick y'know, Put a bit of after shave on and toddle off down to reception with your flip flops and 'Take That' boxer shorts on. You could tell him you've twisted your ankle or something. At least you're not kicking his back doors in bro!"

"Don't fucking bro me. I can't play loose to a gay Spic security guard. What if he's been on the Charlie and starts getting all frisky err. Shane I can't do it mate."

"Well, we're going to have to lure him into the apartment, fill him in and hide him in the refrigerator until I get on the plane."

"We can't fill him in and hide him in the fridge Shane, get a grip."

"I tell you what Nobby, some fucking mate you are. There are loads of police cars that keep going up and down this street. It won't be long before they've located my whereabouts, then what, eh….eh?"

Nobby walked across to the other side of the room. "They're not Police cars, they're taxi's dropping people off at their apartments. Look," he snapped back, pointing off the balcony.

"That's bollocks mate, they're just disguised so we don't see them coming trust me, I'm not falling for that one, no way."

"What, so all of the Police cars in Tenerife have just changed into taxi's because you might recognise them? Fucking hell, come off it."

There was a noise outside. I hid behind the door then underneath the bed, under the table and back behind the door again.

'Bump Bump Bump.'

"Hola, La puerta, la puerta." Sounded a Spanish voice saying 'the door'

This was it I was fucked. The police had located me and now I'm proper deep in the shit. Nobby stood close to the door with his eyes popping out of his head and a face the colour of a bottle of milk. "What shall I do Shane?"

"This, is not funny," I told him as his face changed colour once again.

I think for a split second he'd started to believe what I had told him.

"Don't fucking' answer it, they might fuck off." I whispered

The door didn't go again.

It was around 6ish. Nobby and I had sat up for what seemed like ages trying to work out how to act if it did go pear shaped.

Things got a little out of hand when I came up with going back to England on a jet ski because they only carry enough juice for an hour or so which would have left me in the middle of the Atlantic Ocean without a paddle. Nobby was trying his best to talk me down. "Let's just wait a little longer Shane ok?"

Ten Prozac and a bottle of 'Blow your bollocks off vodka' later, I agreed.

"Ok Nob, not too long though eh?"

He shook his head in relief.

The dark started to change into light. All I could picture was a load of tourists finding arms and legs on the beach this morning whilst making sand castles and stuff. It was a horrible horrible feeling.

The light took over the dark and as it disappeared I'd hoped that the bad feeling would have gone with it, but it didn't.

"Listen Nob, I got an idea."

"Oh no, what now? Don't tell me, we should kidnap the receptionist hide her in a carton of Benson and Hedges then we could post her to another country and no one would ever know.

"There's no need to be sarcastic y' cunt. What a stupid idea anyway, Bensons, please."

For the second time we could hear voices at the front door.

"Been around the world and I I I, I can't find my baby. I don't know and I don't know why, why she's gone away…"

It was Hort singing his favorite Lisa Stansfield song. The door swung open.

"Oi Oi lads, you brought no women back? I don't know, you've either got it or you haven't. What the fuck happened to you Shane, you were in a right bad way?"

I pulled him to one side so that the girl he was with couldn't hear us. "Hort listen to me very closely. Did you see anything last night after I'd left the club?"

He shook his head. "There was a fight at the burger stand, but nothing out of the ordinary. You were well para about something, but you definitely weren't fighting. Two young blokes who we were chatting to in Tramps said that they saw you crawling on your hands and knees by a parked car early this morning with a huge bush sticking out the back of your shirt!"

Nobby started giggling. I'm not sure if it was a nervous one or not.

I looked down with my hand on my forehead. "Honestly?"

"You were right about that bit then," Nobby said.

I looked back at Hort. "What else did they say?"

"I think you were just on a Para attack, you didn't do anything wrong. Don't worry." Hort replied.

As much as I wanted to believe Hort there was a man in my head saying

'You did, you did." There was nothing 100% that could convince me that I did do it, but there again I could say the same for I really didn't.

Nobby explained that I was going to hide the security guard in the fridge and fuck off back to Brum on a jet ski which Hort and his bird found absolutely hilarious.

Our flight left the early hours of the next morning so I decided to try to get some sleep.

I can't remember much about the trip back to Birmingham. I was standing in the queue to go through security at the airport and found a lump of hashish in my coat pocket. I didn't want to throw it away so I ate it instead.

Apparently I was told that half way through the flight I'd woken up and couldn't stop laughing. Everyone on the plane became more and more agitated as I laughed and cried with rib tickling pain for a good hour or so, and then I passed out.

Elvis, who had spent the whole week deliberately avoiding any contact with the sun so that his dear beloved would think he'd been to the Isle of Man to change his passport, finally got home. He sat down as pale faced as when he had left and explained what sort of a week he'd had. He then toddled off upstairs to bring down the presents for his missus.

It wasn't the presents themselves that were the problem as he'd carefully selected such to take her away from the scent. The problem was it was all too late when he'd plonked them down on her lap with a smug grin to go with it. This quickly changed when she pointed it out to him that the currency in the Isle of Man was not pesetas like the stickers said and the carrier bags read **'I LOVE TENERIFE!'**

Jim Frensham

John & Julie

Meet The Boys

Me, Joelean, Giles, pat, Mitch & Claire @ The Japonese restaurant, Tenerife.

Me and Our Beck

The Family Hol's with Carol, Bill, Janis, Brian, Nicola, Dad, mom, John, Joan and Grandad Meacham

The Terminator

Mom & Dad

Mom & Dads Wedding Day

Megan & Emily

Eatin crusts makes your hair go curly!

'Waddya mean there's no Jagermeister left?'

My Mexican Beach friend

The Struggling monkey Bar staff, Gemma & Laura

ROYAL JUDGE BALTAZAR GARZON

On the first of February 2005, we were called out by the functionario in Tenerife II penitentiary and were told that we were being shipped, by prison boat, to mainland Spain.

Royal judge, Baltazar Garzon had indeed fully accepted our case and 'officially' we were now being charged with Currency forgery and international organized crime.

Eighteen months had passed by yet still we hadn't been to trial. We were still at instruction level which means the case was still under investigation. This is the British equivalent to being in the police station shortly after arrest!

Levente Nagy, one of my co-accused from Hungary and I spent three days on a prison boat from Santa Cruz in Tenerife north to Gran Canaria and finally we headed across the Atlantic Ocean. We reached Cadiz port in the Spanish mainland where we were thrown in a 'meat wagon' by the Guardia civil and driven to C.P. Cadiz, Puerto Santa Maria.

This was a start of a week's journey which included stays at some of Spain's most notorious penitentiaries to include C.P. Badajoz in Extremadura, C.P. Topaz in Salamanca, and last, but by no means least General Franco's stronghold C.P. Valladolid in Villanubla. The sunny warm climate of the Canary Islands had dropped drastically to northern Spain's, -15 degrees with very very cold wind chill factors. Along with it we found ourselves staying five up in a cell in Badajoz. The conditions here were unbelievable. All of the walls were smeared with shit and snot which showed us of the 'toe ragged' prisoners who'd already had the pleasure of staying there before us. A small toilet or hole in a plank sat in the corner of the ice cold cell, caked with shit clumps and over spilling with dark brown stagnant piss which reminded me of un-serviced public toilets back home. The prisoners who we'd mixed with on our trip up north looked horribly haggard and worn out. The majority of them hadn't seen water in months and stank like old tramps who'd been sitting on benches all their lives with bottles and cans of booze trying to keep warm.

The screws were proper horrible bastards and went out of their way to make things extra difficult for the foreigners especially on receiving their answer to, *'where are you from?'* They would normally fire back with 'Ah Inglish eh? Well you're not in Ingland now eh'

Another one was 'What happened in Gibraltar' which was a snide remark for their remembrance of the 'Brits' kicking 'Spic' ass a few hundred years ago when we sunk their apparently 'Invincible Spanish armada.' (It's not our fault if the twats can't fight is it?)

Before you enter the main wings of the prisons in Spain you have to go through what they call 'ingresos' which is an isolated block where you could be waiting for up to 2 to 3 days whilst the system processes your details, medical status and whether you are condemned or remand. This part of the prison takes all of your belongings tips them out on the floor and searches for sharp implements, prohibited items etc. After that you are strip searched, metal detected and told to repack all of the mess the screws have made of your belongings. Believe me after the first time this really pisses you off. We went through six in one week.

Levy and I were processed, photographed and informed by the Educador (educator) that we were allocated to modulo number 4.

The electric doors opened and allowed us in to the wing where the screws offices were. Same old shit name, ID card, where are you from. Our clothes and mattresses and bedding followed us is with a Spanish John Inman look alike from 'Are you being served' "I'm free".

We were told that we were to move to cell number 36 on the second floor as the doors opened and allowed us onto the wing. We then received the normal curiosity treatment which was given to all the 'new kids on the block'. The prisoners would normally crowd around staring and whispering. The majority of the people here looked on the brink of pneumonia. Woolly hats, scarves and big coats with two, three, four jumpers. Man, was it cold.

Jamus, another one of my co accused who had traveled two weeks prior to us shook his head. "Fuck me they've really stitched us up this time."

We all sat together in the refrigerated dining hall and ate the best of the decrepit offerings that had had been served up by the dirty heroin addicts. You could feel the people stare and I assured Levy that it was for no other reason than we were the only people in the jail with our own teeth. This brought a temporary smile, which in this hell hole was all we were going to get by the looks of the other inmates drawn looks.

It was the 7th of February when we first entered Valladolid. Summer was months away and our cells were the closest thing I have ever slept in next to a deep freezer. At some point we must have had some kind of heating in this place, as a powerful fan blasted ice cold air in through the ducts, which I suppose was once hot until the fucking thing burnt out.

One thing for sure was, that much longer in these conditions and the fan wasn't the only thing that was going to be burnt out (The pen goes down as I turn over to try to sleep, with a hat and four jumpers on in this fucking fridge!)

On the 6th of March 2005 we were moved, yet again, to another prison. This time closer to the centre of Madrid where the 'Audiencia National' is situated, we were asked to re declare because we had now moved up to a higher court. Although Valdemoro was a bad shithole, we preferred it to the northern concentration camp. There were people there who you could have a decent conversation with and unlike Valladolid some of the inmates were English. I called the embassy and told them our reasons for wanting to stay closer to Madrid. As usual they couldn't help us. The British have no power in the Spanish judicial system. They also informed us that we were the only two British citizens to stay in this Nazi penitentiary in all of the thirty years it had been standing.

Four weeks later we were all back in Valladolid once again. The weather had become a little milder, but our hopes at this point were riding low. In three months time we'd completed two years on remand, the case was still open, and there was still no new evidence since our arrest. It didn't seem to bother the courts that they didn't have enough evidence to finally prosecute us for false money and in that case the next charge down was forgery of public documents which we had already completed enough time on remand to cover us. If you stay in prison on remand in Spain for half of your maximum possible sentence, the courts have to release you on bail, pending a court appearance.

The next three months dragged. If it hadn't been for the visits of my good pal Steve Pettitt I don't know what I would have done.

The prison after this long two years on remand had mentally started to take its toll on all of us. It's a combination of deception , lies and not knowing whether you're going to walk out the door tomorrow or wait another two years on remand and get slammed with a 'fifteen stretch' for the fucking face, which in our case was becoming a possibility. They had closed down my nightclub, seized my Porsche and frozen both my bank accounts and still not showed me any evidence of what they had on me. Normally, people get dealt with within two years, but we had now been categorized with major drug traffickers, terrorists and monetary offences against the government which meant we could 'legally' be waiting for 4 years on remand before they told us if we were guilty or not.

We called our lawyers every week for any news of movement, but every day when we could get through we were told nothing had changed.

On the 23rd of July, we were once again told to pack all of our belongings and prepare to move back to Valdemoro in Madrid to appear at court. As well as entering a prison, you also have to go to ingresos on the way out. This time around the heating was fully operational and I couldn't quite grasp what it was, but for the first time in some time I felt at ease. It was as if we'd come to the end of our misfortunes and things were going to get better for us. Maybe as our two years were up on the 16th of August they would take us to court and bail us, as the case wasn't that strong?

A few weeks ago on TV there were 17 Romanians 'nicked' for loads of shit. 200 credit cards, 6 computers full of information on disks and 4 million Euros in fake euro notes. Surely we would be considered small fry in comparison I thought.

The meat wagon turned up at 7.30 on Friday morning. We were given a bottle of water and a spam roll to scoff on our 350km journey south.

On the meat wagon they transport you down there in twenty small sweat boxes which are laid out ten either side, with a shoulder width alley in the centre for access. Near to the front of the wagon and to the right is the toilet. Each tiny cabin is just wide enough for two people to squeeze in and you have half an arms length in front. As always the walls and ceilings are plastered in snot and spit and smell like Steptoe's jockstrap.

The journey itself was very noisy and bumpy. We stopped at C.P. Topaz to collect other prisoners who had also been summoned to court.

To our surprise we were due in court the next day and all of us suffered from butterflies, as we were sure as ever for a possible release.

This was not to be, and I was met by a duty solicitor who told me twenty seconds before entering into the court room, not to say anything except that I had family, and business in Spain.

The judge stared at me for a moment and flicked his cigarette in the ashtray. The instruction court rooms in Spain are nothing at all like in England they're more like offices and everything seems real casual.

The prosecutor was unkempt and scruffy, looking through piles of paperwork. The Judge, Fernando Grande Marlaska looked up. "Mr. Lloyd, you are here today to sign for extended remand."

My stomach churned and I felt fucking sick.

He pulled out a document and handed it to the prosecutor. "We consider foreigners in Spain a very high risk for absconding and therefore remand you for a further two years."

That was it, I was told to stand up and leave the courtroom and as I stood I turned to the judge. "But, we're in the European community where can I run to?"

The judge looked up at me. "Don't worry Mr. Lloyd we can only keep you for a maximum of four years on remand then the law says if you haven't been to court then , we have to release you. Goodbye Mr. Lloyd."

We all received similar treatment and in the holding cells under the court the doors and walls were getting a kicking. The court secretary had informed our lawyers that the case was now being closed, which meant we should be in court by this October as, we were moving from instruction level to the final court where the trial would be heard.

We later found this out to be partly true and the case had closed, but our new lawyer from Madrid said that we could still be waiting at least six months for trial. I called her a few weeks on and she told me that she was going to speak with the public prosecutor the first week in September to bring a few things to his attention. For example, there's no evidence and no witnesses, which sounds pathetic that they could even accuse anyone without these important facts, but they do.

Every time we called the lawyer after August we got the same old story.

'The prosecutor was busy, then he was on holiday, studying our case, busy again.' Two more months went by, three, four.

I was. Sorry my friends were paying the lawyer and all I was receiving was blag, blag, and more blag. 'Call me next week' then the phone never got answered and another holiday turned up. Spain has more holidays than any other country in the world and they have them for any reason at all.

Don't get me wrong, as you've probably noticed I love holidays, but if your'e trying to get out of prison and every time you make an attempt for bail a fucking holiday turns up it really pisses you off believe me!.

In Tenerife they have a holiday for the burial of the sardine! What the fucks all that about eh? Another one for the day the Queen farted in public, and the first time the king eat bacon and egg sarnies with Daddies brown sauce on, after a crack binge. Spanish holidays will never be the same to me ever again. My third Christmas is only a few weeks away an I'm told by my lawyer once again that next week, or the one after, because this week there's another fucking holiday, she will be asking the prosecutor for our freedom. She also said that because it's Christmas and the circumstances being in our favour I have a very good chance. Let's see.

SORT IT OUT

The beginning of 1997 started slowly, as do most new years. January was a month of sorting out all of the things that you promised to do before or during the festive season. Little did I know that in six years time I'd be sitting in some of Spain's most dangerous penitentiaries, waiting to go to trial for a possible fifteen year sentence and in the process watching all the things I had worked hard for slip through my fingers, my house, nightclub, cars and much, more.

Christmas in England has always been blown out of proportion. After the eve of Christmas getting absolutely bladdered on anything an everything minutely alcoholic you'd got nowhere to go the next night or the pubs unlike now were always closed at 10pm. After winding up your spirits (literally) it always seemed like a big anti climax for a class 'A' party animal like me.

I started to get bored of the same old routine and towards the end of the month became pre-occupied about a broad spectrum of things, especially one in particular 'Where was my life going at the moment?'

Jim was doing ok with his extreme sports company 'Warped' in Wolverhampton. Stan had recently opened 'Pierre Victoire' French restaurant in the town with Az as the manager and Hort had a car spares place which kept him busy. I needed something to get me out of bed in the morning other than a bird or the police. Jim and I on more than one occasion had chatted about the possibilities of me establishing a private investigation firm. Some time ago I had completed various courses in the workings and strategies involved in such a business and it seemed the way to go. This sort of work was very flexible, paid well and most of all I didn't have to answer to anyone. It also had a touch of glamour to it which appealed to me greatly. I was able to blend into all sorts of backgrounds and had the patter to go with it. The good thing about being in the entertainment game was that that because you're constantly mixing with all walks of life you can easily pick up on their habits, the way they walk, talk, sit and the type of clothing they wear. If you have the ability to mimic these behavior patterns then you're halfway there, as no one will usually query you if you fall correctly into the said category when you're on a 'mission.'

After a few weeks I started putting together the company structure and looking at ways of generating trade. Things had started looking up until one Thursday lunch time I received a phone call. Not just any phone call, but one that would change my life forever....

THE CALL

"Champers?"

"Alright Stan, what's happening mate?"

"Ah, been busy at the restaurant. We've had a couple of office parties and stuff today. What're your plans for tonight?"

"Nothing really, been working myself mate."

"Well its black Ronnie's fortieth birthday today, y' know our chef? And were thinking of going up to the 'Reynolds bar' in Stafford, if you're up for it?"

I pushed my cup of tea to the side of the table and sat up. "Well Stan, you know you don't have to ask twice with me. What time you thinking of leaving and how are we getting there?"

"9:30 and Az is going to drive Ronnie's car," he replied.

"OK Stan," I said, "I'll bell you when I'm on my way to the restaurant."

Ronnie was 6 feet four and built like brick shit-house. He'd done a few years on the club scene and was a sharpish lad with a good sense of humour. 'I couldn't really miss his fortieth,' I thought.

I rang big Neil and we met at the taxi rank in the town at a quarter past.

Stafford was roughly 15 miles away, and when we finally got there I got in for free as 'Pigeon' one of the old doormen from the Dilke worked there on the door. The Reynolds bar wasn't your average dance club. In fact, it wasn't a dance club at all. It catered for more of your older, squarer crew. I hadn't been out for a while and decided to hammer the vodkas straight away because half the people in there already seemed quite 'tanked up'. I don't like to feel left out y' know.

We all had a really good night until 2am when someone passed a now extremely drunk me, a bag of ten pills which were called 'Spice girls' and free trial samples.

"Have as many as you like." they said.

I could hardly open my eyes to see them. "How many girls are there?

"What girls?" Stan asked.

"Spice girls stupid."

"Five," Az said.

"Well five it is then," I told them.

"Shane."

"Shane."

I'd already dropped them into my hand, thrown them into my mouth and swished them down with 'Absolute black' vodka.

"Propa!" Said Az, with a fucking hell giggle.

"Fly me to the moon and let me play amongst the stars.

Let me see what winters like on Jupiter and Mars."

ERNIE

I rubbed my closed eyes and yawned a big yawn just as Hicka came bowling down the stairs with his long johns on. I glanced out of the window.

"Kid, what you been doing?" he screamed.

I'd fallen on the two seater settee and my back was killing me.

"Why Hick, what d' you mean?" I asked, trying to unbuckle my spine.

I looked at the clock in the living room and it read 7:30am. Slightly confused I looked a Hicka and frowned. "Did you come out with us last night Kid?"

Hick and I always called each other 'Kid' and the same applied to my younger brother John. I could sense many points of stress in the tone of his voice this time around.

"No kid, I stayed in last night. I had an argument with Wendy and she went around her mom's house at about eleven o'clock. Don't you remember coming around here this morning? Fucking' hell kid, look at the state of all the gardens," he told me.

Pushing my face up against the cold window, I looked out. There were loads of gardens with their fences knocked down which had been smashed to smithereens. The once tidy grass and neatly pruned flower beds had become more like motorcross dirt tracks. Smashed glass and broken indicator lenses gave the tell tale signs that some kind of vehicle had done the damage.

I looked back at Hicka. "Don't tell me I did all that kid. Please don't tell me I done that." I pleaded.

"Kid, you did do that…in a fucking milk cart kid!"

I giggled a very nervous giggle.

"Ww ,Wha, what d' you mean, a fucking milk cart Hick?"

What he was about to tell me, I still don't believe to this day.

"Kid, last night, well half past four this morning, you came flying on to our housing estate, doing 100mph handbrake turns across all of the gardens in a big brown diesel milk truck. You'd got no shirt on, a milkman's cap with badge on the front. The tunes were blurring out of both wound down windows and you were 'gurning' like the milk had came from you kid!"

"But, I kid....."

"Then kid," he said

"What there's more?" I was having a nervous breakdown.

"Then after you'd broken down every fence in the neighborhood, you went on a 'charity mission' and delivered milk, cheese, eggs and orange juice to at least forty houses on the estate!' Hicka leaned against the grate with his legs crossed. "Mrs. Wilkes, the divorcee from number 72, I thought she'd had a cardiac arrest."

"For fucks sake, don't say that Hick. Is she ok, what did I do to her?" I said, finding it hard to take it all in.

"It was more a case of what did she do to you. Her front door closed behind you both and you came back half an hour later with lipstick around you dipstick. What the fuck did you take?"

I explained to him that we'd gone to the Reynolds bar and that I remembered being guinea pig to the testing of some 'Spice bird' pills.

"I can't remember anything else Hick, honestly. Where did I park the milk cart then?" I asked him.

"You parked it on 'mad Johns' flower bed underneath the front window and shortly after five police cars and a helicopter were all over the place. I think you robbed it from Stafford kid. One of the neighbours who spoke with the police was told that it had been taken off a milkman in the early hours."

I turned around and went to the kitchen for a glass of water. "I think I was with Stana. Give him a ring Hick."

He called Stana and I stood behind him as he explained the whole rigmarole.

Stana said. "We were pulled over by Stafford drug squad, who were undercover and patrolling the area. Ronnie, had too many to drink and refused to let anyone else drive, he was all over the shop. Anyway, we all got out of the car and Shane started to kick off big time with the old bill telling them to mind their own businesses or he said he'd lynch them all. The police were being very helpful, but he was off his cakehole on 'Spice Girls' and having none of it. One of the officers drove us in Ronnie's car towards the police station to see, if when breathalysed, any of us could have driven back and that's when Shane jumped out of the car window at 50 mph! We were all sitting in the 'Cop shop' when an emergency fax came through. Apparently a local milkman was in the back of his cart sorting out the morning's deliveries when Shane appeared and decided he was going to hi jack the fucker. They reckoned he drop kicked the milkman out of the side loading door and fucked off in it at high speed!"

Hicka was in stitches. "Hang on a minute Stan I'm going to piss myself," he said, dropping the phone and darting to the toilet. He returned shortly after, looked at me and shook his head.

"Then" said Stana, "One of the policemen asked us where he lived in Walsall. We all denied any knowledge of it, but they knew it was him straight away because it had happened only 100 meters away from where he'd jumped out of the car. They remembered us calling his name when we were trying to calm him down from attacking the policeman and ran a check and got him that way."

Hicka turned around. "They've got your details kid!"

That's all I needed. I was already banned from driving for five years. For sure I'd get a six monther at least for driving whilst disqualified the third time around. I can't be going back to jail again, summers just around the corner. 'Oh fuck,' I thought what next.

I stayed at Hicka's house for a few while things cooled down a little. Stan called me and told me that two CID had been around to the restaurant asking where I lived and if I'd be popping back at any specific time. They were both given the old 'I haven't got a clue' treatment and off they went.

I hadn't been registered at my dad's house for some time but for sure they'd be watching close by.

I moved from Hicka's to Stana's house, then from Stana's to Jims. I was getting really tired of moving around all the time it made me feel uprooted.

"I'm going to fuck off to Tenerife Jim. I've had enough of all this shit mate, its tiring me out."

"You're going to have to raise some dough then Champers to get yourself stabilised over there." Jim replied.

The five bedroom house I lived in had to be emptied. There wasn't much there, but I could probably raise a couple of 'grand' or so by flogging bits and bobs. Then I had the cars. Three quick sales in the Bargain pages at a monkey a piece. That makes over two bags of sand.

"Yes Jim Tenerife it is bro."

SOLVENT ABUSE

Come mid week, I had shifted most of the stuff from the house and on the Saturday morning I went into the town on a couple of all day benders with Az and Stana.

I took a girl back home who I'd known for some time and we both dozed off on the second floor of the big three story house I lived in.

It had started to get a little chilly later on and I got up and switched the gas fire up full only to find out that the meter had run out of tokens. I staggered out of the door and headed towards the garage to reload with tokens and shortly after, returned slotting fifteen pounds worth into the grey box. The red light flashed and the wheel started to spin again quite quickly. I raised an eyebrow and made my way back up to the second floor of the house where I emptied the carrier bag of sweets, cigarettes and drinks onto the bed. For some strange reason I wasn't so bothered about the cold now as the trip had warmed me up and I didn't feel it anymore so I just got back underneath the duvet.

A couple of hours later my arm dropped to the side of the bed as I scanned the floor for a lighter, to spark up a smoke. 'I'm sure I'd put it down here somewhere.'

I got back out of bed and made my way towards the kitchen which was along a ten meter long hallway and to the rear of the house. The cooker was electric and the rings took ages to warm up so I lit up my cigarette on the electric toaster instead.

Over the period of about ten hours I repeated this process at least a dozen times. Zoe stayed glued to the bed and seemed somewhat pale faced. Maybe it was the booze warring off I don't know but we both felt very lethargic. I walked into the other room where I'd been earlier, to discover a hissing sound coming from the facing wall. My heart missed a beat, as I stood frozen to the spot for a split second realising what had happened and what still could occur.

The gas fire had indeed been switched on full for the past ten hours unlit. I slowly walked over towards the window and opened the latch like a bomb disposal expert would on a mission. My hand hovered close to the light switch and then quickly returned to my side.

'Why hadn't I switched the light on for the past ten hours?' It had been quite dark most of the time, and what about the strange missing lighter making me travel along the other side of the big house to arrive at the kitchen, to light a dozen cigarettes or so from the electric toaster?

Crouching down by the side of the bed I noticed the glimmer of the chromed metal lighter sticking out at the side of a can of Coke. One flick of that baby and there wasn't a single doubt in my mind that at present inside this huge place was enough gas to blast my house, and the two houses either side clean off the face of the earth!

Every window became quickly opened, and the house became fridge like once again. No wonder we'd become pale and lethargic, breathing in fifteen quid's worth of British gas.

It wasn't something that I'd think of all the time, but I was sure that someone 'up there' was looking after me on that day!

I M A CELEBRITY GET ME OUT OF HERE

Big Neil had decided he could do with a holiday and after plucking up enough courage to join me, we both booked a fortnight 18 to 30 holiday in Tenerife south's Playa de Las Americas. The flight was a week away on a Friday, so we had plenty of time to prepare and it gave me enough time to tie up any loose ends.

I off loaded the three motors to my 'Biker friends' and had collected enough money to be able to relax while I looked at the options I had on offer, living on this alien island in the middle of the Atlantic Ocean.

The police had informed a relative of mine that there was a large quantity of cash stolen from the truck and it wasn't so much the theft of the vehicle that they wanted to clear up, but what had happened to the cash"

I took a train and headed down south for a few days to think a bit straighter without the worry of getting my collar felt. Being as I'd had a taste of Tenerife before, be it somewhat a small one, I could earn my bread and butter by selling stuff to drunken tourists in the middle of the night. Glow sticks, flashing pendants and anything party like which would attract the goggle eyed, I thought. I found a company that day and ordered a grand's worth, delivered into the Canaries. The company informed me they would be at my feet in a fortnight. Sorted.

I'd only been down south two days and Zoe started getting pissed off with all the attention I was receiving from the normally bored local girls who had never seen the likes of a party animal like me before.

I called Stana. "Alright mate, I'm on my way back up north to the real world. I've got too many women problems down here for my liking. I've never met a bunch of squares in my life. The boozers are like mortuaries. If you pull a fifty out down here the locals think your giving it the 'big un' and start getting moody with you. I'll see you in the morning." I told him.

I said my goodbyes to all and made another 300 mile trip back up north.

It was Thursday now, and tomorrow at 10:30 my plane left the unpredictable weather of England for 365 days a year of guaranteed Canarian sunshine, pussy on tap and enough pills and powder to get Ozzy Osborne out of bed. Wicked!

We stayed up through the night chatting about what I was going to do over in Tenerife. I'm quite sure that the majority of them thought I would have been back the following week if the truth had been told, but I didn't have any intentions of returning. I was really going to miss them all and their ways. Lotty sat there and grinned all night off the powder and pill cocktail she'd been prescribed earlier. She always wore her sunglasses when she was too 'off it' so she could hide away and drift off into 'Lotty land' whilst snuggled up to Jim.

The clock chimed seven and we had to be at the airport at least an hour before takeoff. I shouted Jim who'd dragged Lotty upstairs feeling frisky.

"Don't ye be worrying," he told me, in a broad Scottish accent.

I've heard that one before I thought, recalling what had happened at Heathrow last time.

It was nine o'clock, but still no movement. I was ready to roll and full of butter flies. Jim managed a couple of grunts and went for a shower at a quarter past. At a half past we were just ready to go, loaded up the Land cruiser and off we went.

I looked around at Jim from the passenger seat. "Bro, I should have been clocked in at …. Well fifteen minutes ago. How long does it take to get there?"

"Shane, chill. I've turned up fifteen minutes before take off and they've let me on." He replied.

At ten past ten we all rushed in towards check in. The girls were about to leave when I gave them a shout. We struggled to put our point across about the imaginary traffic jam, but with Jim and me both on the case we got finally through to them.

The stewardess handed me the travel documents. "Your extra tall friend is in the departure lounge waiting for you Mr. Lloyd. Your boarding gate three upstairs opposite the escalator," she informed me has I darted.

"Mr. Lloyd."

"Mr. Lloyd, your tickets."

I span back around. "Oh yeah, that'd be useful, cheers."

Hugs and kisses were exchanged, I made my way passed security and I gave a final wave to Jim and Lotty.

Within a few minutes I'd found Neil. It was as easy as finding the giraffes at the zoo. He threw his hands in the air. "I didn't think you were coming. There was loads of 'old bill' hovering around at the check in desk until ten o'clock. I'm sure they were waiting for you, honestly."

"Let's go and sit somewhere out of the way then mate. You're making me paranoid man."

We moved towards the food outlets where it was a little more busy and easier to hide. I'd got this far. To be collared now would be a big shame.

Gate 3 opened and we boarded. I was still a little worried that the 'Feds' would get me from off the plane. The door closed and off we went. I breathed a sigh of relief.

FANTASY ISLAND

At 2:45 the plane had descended enough for us to be able to see the island. It then took a hard 180 degree turn to face the southern airport called Sofia Reina.

The speaker crackled above my head. "Good afternoon ladies and gentlemen, this is your captain speaking. In approximately five minutes we'll be making an approach into Sofia Reina airport which at the moment has a temperature of 43 degrees centigrade. I hope that you've enjoyed flying with us and we wish you all a very happy holiday. Thank you for flying with JMC.

We hit touchdown and I greeted my now new home with glee. That was it now. No way would the British police find me here. We collected our luggage and headed to the way out sign. The automatic doors slid open and loads of reps stood there all with notice boards in the air.

Neil pointed over my head. "There it is."

A fit blonde bird stood a few metres in front of us with a club 18 to 30's board. She ticked off both of our names from a list and told us to go for coach number seven. We took a few steps forward and I became intercepted as I passed through the second set of sliding doors. Two men in white shirts and red ties stood in front of big Neil and me.

"Excuse me sir," Said the broader one of two. "Are you Shane Lloyd?"

I broke out into a cold sweat. These people were not from Tenerife, they were Brits and they couldn't be from the airlines because they already knew I was on the plane. So I immediately assumed they were Coppers. I slid my passport from my back pocket and slyly passed it to Neil. If their next question wasn't to my liking I was dropping the nut and fucking off.

"Yes I am, why?"

"Well did you have any problems getting on the plane in the U.K., because according to our records you shouldn't have been on the flight?"

I folded my arms." No, did I fuck! Anymore questions?"

"No, that's all." He replied, looking at his friend and shrugging his shoulders, as if to say he didn't understand.

Neil had been 100% right about the police at the airport. They'd obviously informed someone that I wouldn't be traveling and that if I turned up I'd have been going with them. They'd waited until ten o clock at the check in, thought that I was on to them, and fucked off.

'Who the fuck had told them I was getting on this flight and the time,' I thought? I became very puzzled at how they had found out the travel info. I mean ,come on, I'd robbed a van to get a lift home. They'd got the fucker back with hardly any damage, so what's the big deal then. It's not as if I'd robbed a bank or murdered someone is it? I couldn't understand for the life of me why I'd been tracked half way across the globe for next to nothing.

We spent a week at hotel 'Vina del Mar' and did all the things that tourists do, including getting ripped off on the party excursions after paying a 'score' for three drinks and a load of silly games. Once bitten, twice shy I say.

I brought a Spanish Mobile and after a few hours of messing with all of the buttons I got it to display in English. Texting all of my friends the new number made me feel closer to home. On last few nights of the holiday I made a point of asking around for accommodation. It was going to be expensive going solo so I needed to get it sorted ASAP.

On the last day I still hadn't found anywhere to stay. Gareth, my mate from a group called 'Outrun' who were also from Walsall, tried for me too, but everywhere was full.

"Try at the row of hotels next to the 'Cabaret 2000' strip bar," said one PR who'd been staying there shortly before.

It was the morning of our last day at Vina del Mar. We packed all of our stuff and headed downstairs to get our final, full English breakfasts.

"Well Neil," I said, "I hope you have a good flight mate and show off your sun tan to all the girls back home."

He seemed a bit pissed off he was leaving. "I wished that I had the bollocks to stay with you, honestly I do. All of this lovely weather and the smiling crowds. I'm just worried that all of this stuff I've ordered. They reckoned it'd be at my feet in a fortnight. You don't reckon it has been lost do you?"

He shook his head. "You know what it's like once you've paid, they tell you anything. I think you'll get it but it may be a little late. Although this is Spanish territory it'll have to go through two lots of customs for the Canaries. You'll just have to be careful with your money until your rolling that's all. That Mark from Leeds the PR told me yesterday that the small hotel around the corner was around 5000 pesetas (twenty quid) a night. You could use that if all else failed." He said.

We polished off our breakfasts and carried our luggage down to reception. The coach we were told would be arriving in forty minutes so we both sat on the wall outside for a while and Neil caught his last few rays.

Finally it came and I helped to load his luggage onto the hot smelling diesel coach. The rep came over with a clip board. "Is there a Shane Lloyd here? Shane Lloyd anyone?" she queried.

"You need to be careful mate, they're onto you big time," Neil said.

Without a doubt, the police were planning on nicking me back in rainy old England on my return. Shame I wasn't going back though eh? I thought.

The rep walked over to Neil and looked me in the face. "Are you Shane Lloyd?"

I shook my head. "No love, I'm not. I'm just helping this gentleman on the bus with his luggage."

She looked up at Neil. "But you flew here with Mr. Lloyd though, right?"

"Yes I did, but he went missing a few days ago and I think he's now staying with a girl," he answered.

She walked away informing another rep who raised his eyebrows then shrugged his shoulders in reply to her. Quickly throwing the bag I had onto the coach, I shook the big fellows' hand. "Right then Orange peel, it's a bit 'hot here' for my liking, I'm off," I said with a smile.

"OK," he replied, "You look after yourself." And I toddled off down the pathway towards the reception car park.

ARE YOU LONESOME TONIGHT

There was no television, and the shower head spilt out water like a dripping tap, but other than that, for just over twenty quid a night I couldn't really complain. It wasn't too far away from the busy nightlife so I didn't have to spend any more dosh on taxis, and it gave me a little time to stabilize myself. I lay on the bed for an hour or so with my eyes closed listening to the radio and as I lifted my hand to scratch I felt something move.

There was a huge cockroach sitting on my chest with big brown armor plated wings and antenna protruding from its ugly deformed head. I quickly jumped up and made one of those noises that people do when these things take you by surprise. I hate creepy crawlies at the best of times, especially giant foreign ones, they stop you from relaxing unless they're squashed and then you still can't help thinking there are more can you? I spent the next hour and a half 'cockroach hunting', and then I took a walk to the shops to buy some spray to dowse under the sinks and in the bathroom.

Come eight o' clock I was all fidgety and needed to go out. I always liked time on my own in England, but this was different knowing that your real friends were miles away and a short call would cost a fortune. It seemed to amplify the detached feeling.

I fed my face for two pounds fifty, and then decided to take a strole around and get used to my new surroundings. I found it quite difficult to take in all of the info around me and became easily distracted with the screams and shouts from the holidaymakers enjoying their vacations. This wasn't going to be as easy as I thought.

I spent the next two months standing on the doors talking to the security at different bars and clubs. These are the people who know what's going on in the area. They stay on the doors all night long watching folk go backwards and forwards. They know who runs what and who sells what and also where the boarders for the different groups are, if any. Luckily enough for me I had an almost professional knowledge of the interests of probably 90% the doormen on the island 'Anabolic steroids. I never failed to raise eyebrows when I started to come out with high-tech quotations about the new 191 amino acid growth hormone, how steroid cycles should be correctly performed, how to use insulin and the proper way to feed the muscle proteins. Every time I spun the lines to a new found friend the doors began to open.

Three months passed by, but still no parcels had been delivered to me. I'd spent the best part of a hundred pounds on calls trying to find out what'd gone on. In the end they agreed to deliver another identical parcel in England to replace the lost one.

Only two days later I received the delivery number for the original parcel which I collected and denied all knowledge of touching it. Two for the price of one sounded good to me now the cash flow had lowered substantially.

It was now October and the busy summertime was slowly coming to an end. Many of the workers were going back to England for Christmas to detoxify from the colossal liver and kidney bashing that they had subjected their once healthy bodies to. I used to find it quite amusing that some of their parents had actually sent them to the island to get them off the drugs and to help them get a fresh start. Not some, but all of them returned home ten times worse than when they had left.

By the end of the year I had recuperated the money back from the parcel and had enough left over to start a few more ventures. I bought a desk top computer and started to supply all of the bars with publicity stuff Printed shirts, flyers, stickers and anything else that could be designed on computer. I hadn't previously been taught how to use a pc, but seemed to pick everything up at hyper speed.

THE KNOCKING SHOP

The beginning of 1998 was hectic. I had to move apartment for the two weeks over Christmas, as Roberto our landlord handily rented ours out during the most expensive part of the year, which left my lodgers and I homeless. I had an offer to stay with Darryl and Lynwin who I'd known since landing on the island. I lodged with them until the middle of January. I think Daryl's girlfriend was sad to see me go, as 'it hadn't stopped snowing' since I'd got there' he said she'd once mentioned.

April I moved into a two bed roomed apartment in Pueblo Canario (Canary village). Mark, one of my lodgers went on a paranoia trip after a fight in Veronicas and left for England in fear of reprisals. Ashley stayed with me, and then Welsh Joe's dad passed away and he had to go back too.

The apartment was easily capable of sleeping seven, so to cut down costs I decided to take in lodgers. My house rules were quite simple. The occupants had to be between 17 and 25, female, slim and British! Within a fortnight I had a house full of different types of young ladies from all over Britain, Scottish, welsh and English. There were male PR's in veronicas offering to pay double rent for a space on the floor. Bernie and Shelley were Birmingham and Sutton girls who along with Kelly from Camden and Ashley, worked at the Ministry of Sound. Katie was a singer at the 'Full Monty bar' in the Patch and Zoe and another Katie turned up with a cousin whose name I never got to find out. More and more girls would knock on my door until eventually we had ten staying with us and couldn't fit in any more, which made me rent free with profit. There were drunken bodies scattered all over the place, in the kitchen, the balcony, every fucking where. The cafeteria next door, where everyone had to pass to get to the apartment, thought I was a pimp, walking around in my gold Moschino sunglasses with nearly a dozen girls parading backwards and forwards half naked, wrecked out of their minds on everything you could imagine, throughout the length of the day!

'Big Shane' from Runcorn, close to Liverpool and his best mate Dave were security on the doors in various clubs in las Americas. Every night at eleven o'clock, both of them would appear at my place bottles of vodka in hand and a bag full of bugle as a chaser. By this time all of the girls had gone to work and the once noisy house became mine again.

Big Shane, who had always got a grin on his face, came through the front door. "Right, lets have a drink, a go on the playstation, get charlied up and go and fill some cunt in," he said, with Dave smirking behind him.

We'd all sit there, polish off a couple bottles of vodka, waft some devils dandruff, hammer the play station, and off they'd go. Within a few hours they'd appear in Veronicas telling everyone about the fights they'd been in. They just couldn't help it. The row became the drug for them.

In midsummer if there was a pie worth sticking your finger in, my finger was in it. I wasn't the sort of person who would try to get involved in something that half a dozen people were doing because Tenerife was full of sloppy grafters, making mistakes, getting nicked and losing too much kit. After a spell chasing people across the island I gave up and moved to greener pastures.

All I did for the next few months was employ staff to sell glow sticks and necklaces which was a low maintenance job for me, and proved to be quite profitable. The staff were paid on a 'commission only' basis. No work, no pay. It wasn't difficult for them to earn hundred quid a night for the girls who dressed to please. The problem wasn't the selling because in mid swing summer of '98' the streets were flooded with punters wanting to spend their pockets full of dosh .The only thing that people come on holiday for is to smile and have a good time. All you have to do is get them to do both of those things and what they have in their pockets becomes yours. Simple.

For the umpteenth time on a Friday, four of the girls hadn't turned up. The thing was that on a Thursday they always had a good night earning and then decided that they didn't need to work anymore as they'd covered enough for them to not work the next day.

"Listen girls, your days off are on Monday and Tuesday. We're losing too much money on Fridays!" I told them, at a meeting outside the Ministry of Sound.

"Sorry Shane, we went out on a bender yesterday and none of us have had any sleep at all." Said Kelly, puppy eyed.

"Trust me, I've got no problem at all with you going out on benders, but can we try to save them until the beginning of the week thou please?"

It was hard not to go out on benders with so many tourists at it as you felt kind of left out if you didn't join in the fun and frolics. I didn't strong it with them because I could completely relate to what they were saying.

"OK girls, no worries. Just see if you can sort it out next time. Go on then, piss off!" I said with a grin.

The team left and I carried on chatting to two Swedish birds that were in the process of telling me that they'd once been close to making a porno. (Always had time for those girls, don't know why though eh?)

"So then ladies I suppose in this hot climate you must be thinking of trying one out over here soon, right?"

Before I could get my answer a full pint glass came crashing down onto our bench. Both of the girls covered their faces. Some dick head on the level above us at 'Clockwork Orange' had either dropped or thrown it and readily fucked off. Luckily enough all that had been damaged was a few of our drinks and a cut Swedish finger which I sucked better.

Simon and Ricky tuned up with Jeff and a few other Scousers. "Big Shane's upstairs mate, covered in blood from a fight," Jeff said, with a scouse accent.

"Ah, don't worry Shane's always fighting," I replied, still brushing glass from off my once clean shirt.

Jeff started to get panicky. "No mate, this ones a bad one, this mate," and pointed in the direction of Clockwork orange.

I jumped up and flew up the stairs passing through O'Neil's bar.

"What the fucks happened here?" Big Shane was lying flat on his back across a table with his arms and legs hanging over at the sides unconscious. Shortly after, an ambulance arrived and he was put on a drip.

One of the security guards from another bar was trying to mop up the blood which was trickling out of his eye and from around different gashes on his head

"How bad is?" I asked.

"Someone tried to kill him with a spiked knuckle duster. He turned around and the cunt took his eye out with it in the toilet cubicle," He told me.

Lots and lots of people started to crowd around, and in no time he was picked up on a stretcher and placed in the ambulance.

One of the bar owners told me that in his last few moments of consciousness he'd explained what had happened and who had done it.

We turned up at Santa Cruz's Candeleria hospital to find out what had really happened. Shane told us that his attacker was an ex workmate and that he'd been invited into the toilets for a line of Charlie. After his ex, workmate had done a line and Shane bent over the cistern for his, His so-called mate pulled out a large brass duster with a three-inch spike and tried to plough it into the back off his skull. I always say that everyone has his or her time to go and this wasn't his. The spike slid along his skull and didn't penetrate anything but skin. He then received another blow, which was way off target, and as Shane turned around to face his attacker, the third blow plunged straight into his right eye and sunk just millimetres from his brain.

The man then fled, with a waiting lift to the airport, where he was taken straight off the plane and arrested. When the police searched the plane they found 250,000 pesetas (Thousand pounds sterling) which was tucked in the front of the seat that he'd apparently been sitting on and this was logged as being his payment for the job.

All of the local newspapers and TV crews were eager to find out what had happened. Las Veronicas became swamped with police, undercover and uniformed. Cars got burnt out and rumours had started to spread.

No one was quite sure what happened, but the newspapers received notice that the British man locked up in Gran Canaria, had been found hanging in his holding cell at the police station, in suspicious circumstances.

The south of the island was riddled with Chinese whispers once again.

After a short while Shane decided to change his scenery for Magaluf's along with his mate Dave. This was a good move, as I believed that the majority of the people in the south were now being used as 'Cannon Fodder' by various people. It's ok fighting a worthwhile cause, but who wants to risk losing their lives just for the sake of some fucker shouting his mouth off all the time with Julius Caesar syndrome?

SENOR BOND

Working the day shift brought life closer to reality for me. I'd got myself a steady girlfriend and changed somewhat to the extent that I didn't need to go out and play up anymore and I became very content with what I had. Joelean was on holiday when we met and she returned a short time later to stay with me for some years on.

I had recently bought a new speedboat which was moored in Puerto colons 'millionaires' paradise' in the south. We'd both gone to bed early to ensure an early rise for our day out boating and arrived at the port around 7am the following morning. I hadn't actually passed any official boating license courses, but had sufficient knowledge to get me by on an eight meter boat, so I printed a moody license off on computer and left it at that.

We removed the cover and Joelean commented on how 'flash' the red, white and blue leather upholstery looked. The boat became loaded and I started her up waiting a few minutes for the big V8 engine to warm a little.

I untied the front two guide ropes and looked around. "Loose the rope Joe," I shouted, and the boat started to drift out. There were at least another twenty boats in our mooring leg, some much bigger and a few smaller. I nudged the accelerator forward slightly and turned the wheel full lock to the left. The throttle, unknown to me was faulty and had pushed forward more than I had wanted, as result the front end of the boat shot upwards towards the sky with the engine roaring like a race car would at the start line. Joelean gamboled backwards and landed on one of the rear seats. I also went backwards, but managed to grab the wheel in an attempt to steer the now completely out of control boat. We ploughed into the side of a 12 meter cruiser, taking a chunk out of the fiberglass. I pulled back the throttle and the front of the boat hit level once again.

The first thing I did was turn to see if Joelean was ok. She was sitting on the carpeted area at the back of the boat with her hands and feet still in the air, wondering what the fuck had gone on.

"Fuckin' hell darling did anyone see us?" I asked.

"What?" she replied, looking confused and dazed.

I covered my face "Did anyone one see me making a right cunt of myself and smashing into that big 'fuck off' boat?"

I didn't really give a fuck about the boat, but the last thing I needed was for someone telling everyone in the south about the major bollocks up I'd just made pulling my boat out the mooring.

Joe started smiling as I pulled her up off the carpet. "You make me laugh you do."

If that wasn't enough to shit anyone up on their virgin voyage, I don't know what was. We took an hour or so razzing around the outskirts of Las America's coast and later decided to go out to where the whales and dolphins were.

"Darling can we go to La Gomera," she said, pointing to the island which was closest to Tenerife.

"Fuck me Joe; let's get used to the boat first before doing any expeditions eh?" I frowned.

Ten minutes later we were doing 50 knots heading towards La Gomera.

Now, as I'd mentioned earlier, I had a little bit of experience with boats, but on small lakes in England, and all of a sudden found myself belting across the Atlantic, like James Bond, in 40 degrees of sun, with a blonde girl in a high powered speed boat like the 'Rozzers' were after me!

We seemed to be going for ages and as I looked behind me Tenerife's coastline had become none existent, I'd also noticed that La Gomera's didn't seem too close either. I pressed the reset button on the depth finder and after the signal went down to reach the bottom it returned and just read 'DEEP'. I noticed further out that the waves had started to change their movements. They seemed much wider than before and as the boat caught the crest of each wave we drifted some distance to the right and the steering wheel had to be fixed a quarter of a left turn down. At this point I felt a touch nervous, but didn't let on to Joelean, as it was probably nothing. I hit full throttle as to speed up the journey and the big engine powered us down into the lower bowl of one of the big broad blue waves. As we came up the boat flew into the air and its propeller span loudly, freed from the water and the revs seemed to double. We did this for a few minutes and I felt that things were getting a little out of control. The boat had started to make banging noises when it smacked down onto the water, easing back the throttle an inch the Speedo read 35 knots. Even adjusting the power tilt and trim which is a device to level out the ride of the boat, I could still feel the power of the deep beneath us. Joelean turned her head to the right. Her pretty little face and long blonde hair had been drenched from the spray which had been blowing over the front screen. "Bit choppy out there innit darling?" she said, adjusting her sunglasses.

"Just a touch eh," I replied, trying not to look too worried.

The waves seemed to get a little calmer I thought, it was maybe because we were getting into shallower waters. The petrol gauge read ¼ then ½ as the boat swayed from side to side. No worries for juice at the moment. I could see mast tops of boats moored in San Sebastian port. "There's always a petrol station to top up close to the moorings," I told Joe.

"Let's drop anchor close to the beach and do some sunbathing," she said, turning up the stereo so that every cunt in La Gomera knew we'd arrived.

After an hour or so boredom set in so we took a trip to the port to fuel up. San Sebastian was a little awkward to maneuver around because there was a lot of fishing boat traffic constantly coming in and out. La Gomera itself is a small fishing island with ancient morals and a very low population. No way in the world would I ever dream of taking a holiday here, it seemed so boring.

I found a gap in the traffic and slowly floated into the fueling area making sure the crash buoys were level. Then I tied the ropes to secure it.

"Hang on there Joe, I'll be back in two minutes," I said, walking towards the fat ugly man with the scruffy beard who was slumped in a deck chair with flies buzzing around him.

"Hola," I said, dodging a swarm of mosquito's.

"Buenas tardes señor," he replied.

"Nessesito gasolina, por favor."

He took a toke on the half smoked cigar which stayed in his mouth. "No tenemos gasolina aqui. Disculpe."

"What, you've got no petrol?"

A Swedish man came strolling over and after he had a brief conversation with smelly bastard told me that they only sell 'gas oil' which is diesel.

"But fuck me mate, my speedboat is petrol, and I live in Tenerife not shitty La Gomera. What, so no fucker on this island uses petrol. You're having a 'bubble bath' ain't ya mate"

"That's what he says my friend. There is one petrol station about seven kilometers away. If you have petrol cans you could get a taxi to drive you there."

I let out a slow breath of air. "Thanks for your help." I waved and made my way back to the boat.

"Is everything ok darlin'?" Joe seemed to notice there may be a problem.

"Stinky bollox over there said that they only sell diesel and not petrol, so we'll have to go back on half a tank. It's ok though, the gauge read a little under the full mark before we set out and we did a lot of time messing around in Tenerife. There should be plenty enough," I told her.

We pulled back around to one of the beaches and took a bite to eat. It was around two in the afternoon when we'd finished.

"Right then, let's start back shall we," I said, pulling down my base ball cap then pulling up the anchor.

I nudged the boat up to thirty knots and pointed in the direction of Tenerife. After five minutes and as I'd expected the waters had changed again. Something was telling me to go back and return on the ferry. 'It's probably me being silly,' I thought.

Fifteen minutes later we were down to fifteen knots and were experiencing quite strong side winds. I hadn't lowered the throttle, but the currents were against us now and the boat was struggling to go against them and it was zapping our power.

Another ten minutes and our boat had slowed to ten knots, which is around 10 mph. I had to adjust the throttle because at this a stage the waves had started to throw us completely sideways and the steering wheel needed quite some force to turn it in the direction we needed to go in. I took a quick look around, and then a deep breath of the fresh gale that flowed across the huge, huge open blue Ocean that we were in the middle of.

Joelean had changed her position from standing up and peering over the front windscreen to sitting, frequently adjusting herself as the gale blew things out of place. Water had accompanied the wind and now was spraying into the boat from my right hand side. I turned my body to the left with my right knee pushing against the dash boards lower shelf then pointed into the small cabin in between the two seats. "Grab that orange jacket darlin' and put it on. Were ok, but better to be safe than sorry eh?" I told her, in the most relaxed tone I could as not to spook her and let her know that I was getting pretty worried at this point.

She put on her body warmer style life jacket and passed me some other contraption which the zipper had corroded on. I just threw it on the floor. It looked like it would have sunk me anyhow.

A split second later, a huge wave seemed to cover us filling the boat with shit loads of water. I switched on the bilge pump to try to get rid of it, as it was now just below my knees.

"Stay down low." I shouted to Joe who had beaten me to it and was now hiding under the dash board.

"Shane I'm really frightened," she screamed.

"Stay calm darlin, we'll be ok," I screamed back, noticing a huge wave bowling towards us.

How many times have you seen films on TV where people are caught up in storms on small boats in life threatening situations? You could never believe being in a similar scenario.

This time the wave went underneath and in a split second it felt like the floor had disappeared from underneath us. My stomach jolted upwards to the middle of my chest and the back end of the boat, being the heaviest, dropped down first putting us a nearly a vertical angle. Both my hands gripped the water drenched steering wheel and my whole body flew upward as the boat plunged down into the cold Atlantic Ocean.

"Oh god, were going to die," cried Joe, with terror written across her face as she covered her face with her arm.

"Shut the fuck up for god's sake," I yelled back, "If you scare me we will be fucked, now shut it."

Realizing the truth in what I had said she stayed quiet. I wanted to comfort her, but I could hardly blink with so many things coming at us. The last thing we needed was panic because it would have been the end of us both for sure.

We span around so fast that we hit the second wave twice as hard. My knees slipped down the seat and I head butted the edge of the wind screen nearly knocking myself out with blood now pissing out of my skull.

Joe had cleverly wedged herself between the seat and dashboard and hadn't moved an inch. I lifted my seat up and rummaged around. The gun was there, but the only flares I had were in the wardrobe back at home. Another wave hit me in the side of the head temporarily blinding me with the stinging salt and knocked the sunglasses off my face.

The petrol gauge had stopped moving from the empty marker now so 'Are we going to die?' I asked myself.

We hit another wave, another, then another banging really hard as we connected once again with the water, propeller screaming out every few seconds. This all went on for another twenty minutes until I had noticed a pattern in the ocean and started to maneuver the boat how a surfer would his board on a wave. It was working. No more banging or spinning. We were still miles away from land, but at least we had a little more control over the situation. The bilge pump was pumping away the water from the inside and was making a large grinding sort of noise as it worked overtime and the petrol gauge still wasn't moving.

Joelean moved the arm which had been covering her face. "You ok babe?" she said, wiping away water from her eyes.

"Yeah, we're still some way from Tenerife, but it's a little calmer." I told her.

"I thought it was never going to stop. I can't believe it."

"I can't either Joe. That was fuckin' unbelievable. We're going to talk about this for the rest of our lives y' know."

Eventually, the coast of Tenerife became visible once again. My body was covered from head to toe in thick white salt and my skin was red raw from the sun. Tipping a bottle of drinking water over my head I washed my face, pushed back my hair and re adjusted my sunglasses. We entered into Puerto colon harbor and guided the boat into leg number eleven, hosed it down and replaced the cover.

Sitting in the restaurant at the port we didn't speak for 30 minutes and just glared into open space , stunned by the close to death trip that we'd just encountered less than an hour before. We were both completely drained, physically and mentally.

I glanced out the side of my glasses.

"Right then darlin', let's go back out then. Gran Canaria's not much further than la Gomera," I smirked.

TORTURED

On the 1st of January 2006 at 00:10 my father passed away. I was called by one of the screws at the Valladolid penitentiary and was told that I needed to call my brother John, in England on the third of January's afternoon.

Many a time I can remember people saying that you 'knew' when something like this had happened, and you do. It's strange to explain, but you get a sort of 'off frequency' feeling.

My brother told me that he'd had had a funny turn the day before, and he was taken into hospital for observation. The family had stayed at his bedside on New Year's Eve where they had all seen the fresh year in together. I think he hung on for the bells to ring and then peacefully slipped away.

For the few days that approached the New Year, I had hopes of a possible bail grant. Also, I had told myself, on several occasions, that the year of 2006 would see a change in luck for me.

It lasted all of ten minutes.

The social worker at the prison called me out over the loud tannoy and told me that two of my cousins were flying over from England to see me. I was asked to sign a document which verified that I wished them to visit me in Valladolid at any time.

The embassy in Madrid had told Steve and Hicka that everything had been arranged and not to worry. They took time out and booked two flights into northern Spain's chilly Villanubla airport, booked their hotel and made an attempt to contact Daniel Wycombe at the embassy, in Madrid. Despite all of his promises, he'd gone away on holiday and left no instructions with anyone to help them. He, like most of the people in our so called embassy, didn't give a fuck!

Steve and Hicka took a taxi from their hotel to the prison reception and after an explanation of who'd they'd come to see, were escorted inside. After all of the bother that they had gone to driving to Stansted airport, flying, booking the hotel and sorting the taxis, the prison screw at reception told a now extremely frustrated Steve and Hicka that they had a 'glass visit.'

Steve slammed his hand down on the desk. "If that cunt don't call the director now and sort us a 'Vis a Vis' out in one of those rooms over there, I'll string the cunts up!" he told Hicka.

"Too fuckin' right," he agreed.

I explained to the screw that my family had spent lots of money on this journey and I'd signed the paperwork for a room visit (Vis a vis). He came back and told me that no one knew about any 'room visit.'

We took the visit and realising that the Director of the prison had authorized this deliberately we 'flipped our lids' through the glass.

"How can they be such wankers in this situation? The visit rooms are all empty. Can't we sort anything out for later on, or even tomorrow son?" Steve said, hopefully.

The hour went by fast and to add to the frustration we had to shout through the whole to each other as there were no telephones here like in more modern prisons.

I spent all of that afternoon arranging a room visit. The screw told me that it had been sorted. I was so happy and I needed so badly to talk with somebody from the real world. Tomorrow was my dad's funeral and I wasn't going to be in the best of spirit.

The screw called me to the office once again. "Inglish, Tell your cousins to come back to the prison at seven o'clock it's now been authorised."

I called Steve and told him. He told me that the foreign office in London had informed them that no matter what, there was no chance of him getting in to see me.

"But Steve, they've told me here it's all been Ok'd."

"We're on our way then bro. See you in a short while."

Seven o'clock had been and gone, quarter past, then half past eight.

I had sat waiting all this time already stressed to the max thinking of the things I was going to say as not to waste any of the precious time I'd been given.

Steve and Hicka had landed at reception on time, in fact fifteen minutes early. As before they had walked in and explained about the new fully authorised room visit that the Director had just given the ok to. All of the people in reception denied having any knowledge of it and after a few growls from the lads they called the Director who also said he knew nothing about a visit.

They left the prison, jumped in another taxi and after a heavy night on the piss left for England.

It had been some weeks after the funeral and into mid February before I had started to calm down about what the prison had done to deliberately fuck up my head.

The 'Gente Judicial' are the workers who issue legal documents on behalf of the courts. This morning they called me to the office.

Our petition had finally arrived from the Audiencia national. It wasn't as much as we thought it was, but never the less they were asking 8 years for false money and a year for fraud.' Nine fuckin' years,' I thought.

Our lawyer told us that we should be in court before the end of the summer which was around ten weeks away. "Don't worry, they will struggle to condemn you for false money because you didn't have any money or a false credit card," she told me, as my millionth telephone card ran out once again.

In 2002, more and more police were being shipped over from Madrid to cut down the soaring crime rates which seemed to give Tenerife its 'rough and ready image.' It had always been known for its violent side, but the truth was that most of the fights were after 3am in the morning when everyone had passed their 'drink by dates' and the Dutch courage had overwhelmed them to the extent that they had to take off their shirts thinking that everyone thought they were the bollocks. Bright red with a beer belly was always on the conveyer belt passing by in Veronica's as we used to sit and watch the punters go by each night.

I always swore that after so much of the work that I'd done in pubs and clubs over the years that I would never return to that type of work. When I used to speak with my friends on the phone back home many a time they'd ask me ' why don't you open a bar?'

'Too much hard work,' I'd always replied.

Contrary to what I'd said, in June 2002 I placed an amount of money down on a club in Las Americas, which was in Veronica one and in the middle of the tourist zone. The interior was a 'right off' and it had been used as a storage area for some time. I estimated that another twenty grand or so would put it right.

Sods law says 'If it can go wrong it will go wrong.' And it fucking does.

Lots and lots of extra bills were hitting me for re-wiring, air conditioning and every week it seemed like the town hall was bringing out new laws which were costing me dollars. In October, the club was virtually finished and decorated with a huge sound system which could be heard from miles away. The music policy was strictly 'Tuff and Funky House' which went down a bomb, as we were the only club with this style of music in the south of the island. The club took off and raked the money in from day one. Everyone escaped to the 'Crazy House' after dark.

THE BIG FIGHT

On the 4th of November 2002, I planned on taking the night off. My body was telling me to relax for a while as I had given it a bashing a few days before at Miss Moneypenny's when I appeared on Sky televisions 'Tenerife Uncovered.'

The phone rang.

"I'm not going out."

It rang again.

"I'm not going out."

The door knocked.

"I'm not coming out, leave me in peace."

"I've got a headache"

"For fuck sake I've told you a million times, I'm not going fucking out. Leave me!" I screamed.

It went on and on for what seemed like hours.

No matter what I said they wouldn't leave me alone. I even started losing my temper and saying really nasty things to make them fuck off, but they wouldn't take the hint. I switched my phone off and stopped answering the door until it got so bad I agreed.

I took a shower cussing under my breath as I washed my hair in the tepid water. Black trousers and white Armani shirt came out of the wardrobe as I was still thinking about how I could get out of going out.

I couldn't, and didn't want to stay out till the early hours of the morning even if I was offered anything to sniff the answer was going to be no!

The door knocked again and within minutes I found out that I was driving. "Are you taking the piss or what?" I screamed, walking out of the lift. No one else answered, basically because I'd hit the nail on the head.

First of all we ate at the 'Chez Beber 'French restaurant in Fanabe, and after one of them came up the idea of going down to Veronicas I threw my hands up in the air. "I'm not staying down there all night. Just one to say hello and that's it, I'm off with or without you," I said shaking my head that I'd even stood for this much.

We stayed in the Ministry for one and I started to get really tired and fidgety. I needed my bed and didn't want to play anymore. "Right then lets fuck off, I've really had enough now. Say what you like if you don't come with me you'll have to get a taxi home," I said, standing up with the keys in my hand.

We all left the Ministry and as we walked out onto the path, I received a call from someone in mainland Spain.

As we started to walk down to the bottom of the strip, I noticed seven African boys quarrelling about something. I could also see that one of the people I was with was in the middle of it. As I approached them a cleared appeared, which allowed me to enter the widening circle.

All I could here in pigeon English was
"You caan say dat."
"You tell him dis."

I have never feared anyone on this island for the simple fact that I've always treated the people with enough respect to receive it.

I spoke to the one making all of the noise, who turned around and looked at me as if he'd been smoking crack. Lifting his hand and pointing at me at the same time. Things seemed to become very hostile. The people in front of use were immigrants from Nigeria and Senegal and don't really understand the logic of how things should be dealt with on the islands. Because of this, their own lack of intelligence makes them dangerous.

At that, it kicked off!

Twisting slightly clockwise, I span back and landed a right hook clean on the chin of the guy who was in front of me. His head tilted and snot shot from his nostrils as he fell backwards up against the burger van. Between the two of us, these seven were no problem. Their main man was flat on his arse and the rest of them were dropping like flies too. The remaining four just stood back for an instant and for what seemed like a hundredth of a second later around thirty more of them had been teleported around us. Knives were being pulled out, bats, broken bottles and then an automatic pistol, which had been flashed in our faces from the second row of the crowd. This instantly assured me that we were fucked if we didn't get off right away!

I looked up the steep steps to one of the night clubs and saw two more of them running down towards us with clenched fists. 'This is the start of a War' flashed in a millisecond through my mind, with a thousand other thoughts as one of them came straight at me with his arm cocked, ready to strike. I ducked, and punched him hard in the Adams apple, then moved around and rammed the back of his head with my hand, which sent him flying forward. As I quickly turned back around to my left, I felt a hard thud smack me in the in the left side of my face above my cheekbone. I staggered back and looked to see if anyone was helping me, but I was alone. Blood started pissing all over the place and gushed in spurts, inches away from my bludgeoned face. A baseball bat cracked over my head from the back, right hand side, which brought me to my knees, and then the sound of gunfire penetrated my eardrums. My body was riddling with adrenalin and I could have sworn I'd been shot. There was definitely enough blood gushing out of my body to convince me of it. After receiving another two cracks from behind with baseball bats, death became an option.

Glancing to my right, a Spanish woman who was behind the counter in the supermarket started screaming and beckoning me to go inside, furiously waving her arms at me in panic.

I somehow managed to get to my feet and scattered into the supermarket. The woman behind the counter was nearly crying as I looked to the back of the place for an exit or storeroom. There was none.

I took a few deep breaths and slid down a pile of canned foods, looking as I did so for anything that I could use to defend myself with against the thirty or so delirious psychos that had now appeared and were staring at me with broken bottles and bats in their hands chanting.

On wiping some of the blood away, which was still firing out of my face, I realised that I'd been blinded in my left eye with a bottle. I pulled a huge chunk of glass out of the eyeball and another from the gash below it. The ball of my eye had split into two parts and was now bulging out with pain that words cannot explain. If I hesitate half a second too long I'm going to die. People say that your average street fight lasts around twenty seconds and only seems like it's longer. I'd been in this one triple that so far and it looked like I had to do it all again.

Standing along the edge of the entrance to the supermarket I could count eight of the front row had broken bottles all except for the two in the middle, one had a bat and the other was empty handed.

I stood up and growled like a lion. I dropped my head and ran at them like a bull, heading for the three on the left hand side. I was a meter away from them and side stepped quickly through the two centre ones. I figured that there wasn't enough time for him to swing the bat, and at that I split the empty handed ones nose open with a head butt which sent him slamming down to the ground squealing. I barged through all who were blocking the entrance and started to run for my life. My heart was thumping real hard and my lungs were gasping for extra oxygen. I couldn't tell you how many were behind me as a twist of the head to look back could have been the death of me. I reached half way up the road, and had sprinted some fifty meters when I tripped over, and my body went bouncing along the floor.

At least thirty men were kicking and punching at my body and head. A bottle sank in the back of my skull and I scrambled to my feet, still receiving blows as i did so. I managed to run another twenty meters and fell again. I'd lost so much blood I was struggling to function correctly and as I came down this time my wrist and forearm snapped in two pieces. I could feel a stream of warm blood flow down my neck as the blade of something slashed down by my left ear and was followed up by a dozen more boots to the head.

I could feel myself start to lose consciousness and was certain that any moment I was going to die. All of the noises around me seemed to disappear. The punches and cracks from the thirty men didn't hurt anymore, and everything seemed peaceful. This was definitely my last few seconds, I thought.

Out of nowhere, I was injected with a surge of life again. I pulled myself up the trousers of one of the men and bit a chunk out of his face, still roaring like an animal. I still don't know to this day how , but I managed to run another ten meters to safety then collapsed outside the

'Ministry of Sound' where I was met by Sammy, a Moroccan PR who helped straighten my mind out whilst we waited for the ambulance to come. One of the barmaids at the Ministry was an ex nurse. She left the island the next day saying that she'd never seen anything like it in her born days

I was transferred from Hospital las Americas to Candeleria in Tenerife north, the surgeon had informed me that my skull had been fractured in two places. The broken bottle, which had been shoved in my face, had indeed blinded me and my forearm had been broken into bits.

In total, I had over eighty stitches in my face and head and was very lucky to be alive, he also added. I stayed in hospital two more days whilst I had fifteen more stitches in my eyeball to hold it together and then on the third day I signed myself out.

The fracas had hit all the major papers and news on TV. To add to that, on my final day in the Traumatology wing at the hospital the other patients had already seen the news and they greeted me with a round of applause to try to lift my spirits as I walked in.

The headlines read,

'NITECLUB OWNER LOSES EYE FIGHTING 30 MEN IN PUB BRAWL'

Another ten seconds longer it may have read something completely different and I may not have been around to see it.

That's a fact!

The fight had done a lot of physical and physiological damage. The constant throbbing headaches were tearing me apart. Every three hours I had to take Paracetamol, Codeine and a shit load of other stuff to stop infection getting in any of the injuries. The most sensible thing to have done was to have taken a flight to England to recover properly with the correct medical attention. The thing was that the club had only just been opened and I had spent a huge amount of time and money, which needed recovering. I had to stay, or at least until I'd organised everything to cover me for any trip that I did make.

A short while later I decided to close up for some time and go back to England. The people who were hanging around me were untrustworthy. They had started to generate problems with some of my other friends and I was getting the blame for it because they were using my name. I didn't need the hassle. I still hadn't come to terms with what had happened on that November morning.

Back in England, Hicka called me and told me to meet him at the Memorial club for Johnny, his dad's birthday party. Stan came with me and all of the family had turned up for the event. I obviously didn't know at the time, but this was the last drink I would ever have with my dear old dad. We had a good night never the less, God bless him.

Even though I had decided to take time out back home, quite a few things still needed addressing. 'Oliver' my trusty English boxer dog changed home and stayed at a friend's house with a pool and all which upset me lots. He didn't seem too bothered by the change though. The cars went into storage, as they had needed some minor repairs, which left a few bits and bobs to attend to, and all was well again.

Various trips to hospitals and eye infirmary's were unpleasant, but necessary. Finally, I had my last consultation and was on a short list to talk with a surgeon about having an operation. The waiting list was for three months and the surgery was expensive. It was booked and paid for anyway. It wasn't something you could even think about not doing,

Just five weeks away from my operation, an old friend who I had met in Tenerife some years before had contacted me and we decided to take a trip to the island for a short break. I needed to sort out a few things anyway, so we booked our tickets and flew out from Heathrow on a Friday.

We landed at 1am on the 1st of August and took our stretch limo to the posh Mare Nostrum resort in the south. We entered into the reception and were informed by the man at the desk that the two separate rooms we'd booked needed 300 Euros deposit each, which needed to be paid with a credit card.

"Sorry, but we don't have any credit cards," I told him

"Is this just for the mini bar?" Jamus added. If so, then we'll pay for it tomorrow when our stuffs all been unpacked."

The receptionist nodded. "Ok sir no problem," he said, and stood up to show us to our rooms.

"We understand that you are here to enjoy yourselves and have a little party, but please be aware that we have families staying here as well that go to bed a little earlier than you do," he told us, as a young bloke passed us with two hookers wrapped around him.

Jay and I looked at each other laughing at how pissed the kid looked staggering along the hall. Those two pros' would rob him blind as soon as they touched the hotel room. The poor fucker hadn't got a clue had he?

The cases got dropped off and the bell boy got his 50 euro tip.

Within an hour, Winston came around with a bag of green. Nice.

Goodfellows

John Travolta ain't got nothin on our Groove!

Three tough cookies
Steve, Greg & Chinky (Rip)

Greg Pettitt at the Hatton fight in Vegas

Chinky Jones (R.I.P.)

Harrison Pettitt

Britains Hardest Doorman

CANARIAN JAILBIRDS
Levente Nagy (Hungary) Danny O' Connell (London)
Rene Jansen (Holland) & Champers

My Niece Danielle

Dad with Uncle Frank

Debbie O' Grady

Front left to right - Me, John & Paul
Rear Cousins - Wesley, Darren & Dean
BELOW - A young Paul & Maxine.

El Cubano

*Dad fell asleep drunk at a pigeon race.
The one you can see would have won by a mile
If he'd have been awake to time it in!!!
BELOW; On the sesh in Wales*

11 09PM

Was the official time that we were officially 'nicked' at the Police Station in Tenerife south's Playa de las Americas. We'd actually been grabbed by the Canarian 'filth' at around 9:45pm through a routine traffic control check squad, who were operating a few hundred yards down from Lineker's Bar in Starco, Las Americas. As soon as we approached the checkpoint and were some fifty yards away I told the driver to stop the car, and I opened the rear left hand side door.

"I'm not going all through that shit again with the old bill. They kept me waiting 45 minutes last week for fuck all," I said, "I'll meet you in a few minutes at the club over the road."

"Come on mate get back in, we'll just drive through," he told me, as his Hungarian friend Levente nodded in agreement.

I took two steps away from the car. "Nah, I'll walk past and jump back in later. If they see me they might hassle me for fuck all again."

Normally I would have closed the door and just walked away, but I hadn't been feeling in the best frame of mind for some time after my close to death experience, and gave in quite easily to keep the peace.

As soon as I had closed the car door, something told me I had made a big mistake. As the car crawled slowly towards the checkpoint the lump in my throat started to grow. Two cars in front I could see that one of the doormen from Branigans bar who worked for my next door neighbour "Jordie John" had also been pulled over. The police let the grey Seat Ibiza that was in front of us pass by. We tried best we could to stay close to the rear of the other car so as not to get noticed, but the white shirted local policeman tapped on our roof and indicated for us to pull in front of 'Tramps' nightclub.

"Fuck me, I knew it," I said, with my thumb and forefinger on my temple.

The driver opened the door and stepped out of the car. Levente the

Hungarian had just seconds before been given the drivers passport to stick down his bollocks, so if the coppers did look through the car they wouldn't have had any ID to checkout our names against and would have let us go quite quickly.

"Documentos por favor," said the officer in the white shirt, which told us he was local police.

The driver put his hand in his pocket and pulled out an Avis rental car contract and around 1500 Euros in notes. As soon as he'd done it I swore under my breath. What a fucking idiot. That copper's going to wonder why he's carrying so much and where it had come from, straight away.

I stepped out of the car and tried to distract the officer away from it, but two more arrived. The taller one of the two looked at the driver. "Your passport, where is it?' he seemed to be quite pissed off that the driver had more than a month's wages screwed up in his hand. The other officer with him opened the passenger side door of the blue Renault Megane and returned with a passport. The driver glared at the Hungarian who completely ignored what he'd been told to do with the passport and instead had dropped it in the side compartment of the passenger's door.

The tall officer smacked the passport on the back of his hand. "Why you tell me you don have passport, eh?"

The driver stuttered. "I I thought that I'd left it at the hotel."

The police didn't seem to be interested in me at all because I was travelling in the back of the car. I made a point of calling Jamus, who I that I wanted him to move my briefcase documents from the hotel and give them to Tara, she in turn could have taken it to Giles's house. If I did get nicked for anything, the police didn't have to go to our hotel and find anything we didn't want them to. I then put the phone in my pocket. A Grua or recovery truck arrived and shortly after informing the driver that the rental car contract had expired yesterday, started to pull the car onto the back with a steel cable connected to a winch.

The officer, who had discovered the passport sat on the bonnet of a police car examining the tattered red book which looked like it had been washed and also contained an invoice and a green 'Wing hang' bankcard. He had his radio pushed to the left ear.

I lit the cigarette and commented to the Branigans security that what a bunch of pricks the Spic old bill were. I glanced to my right and saw that the driver of the car had started to slip away into the crowds of tourists who were all wondering around looking for somewhere to go for a drink.

The local police officer looked around with a confused expression, his right hand palm down like a DJ with a hand on record. He turned to the Hungarian and poked the 22 stone bodybuilder in the chest.

"Where is your friend," he screamed.

Levente shrugged his shoulders. "I don't know."

The officer turned, muttered something in Spanish to his colleague, explaining what had happened.

I looked at Levy and took a deep breath "Levy, we're fucked now, you know that don't you?

"I know" he replied.

They already had the car half on the truck, so why did the driver fuck off they obviously thought, as another four National police turned up dressed in blue boiler suits. The local copper dashed to the driverside rear door and started to rummage around near the foot well.

"**TARJETA'S,**" he screamed, holding an object out at arms length.

Within seconds, I'd been grabbed by the shirt, punched in the face and neck several times by the Nationals. They all then pulled out shooters and buried them in the back of my neck and back. We were then slammed over the bonnet of a car and had our heads smashed into the denting metal. They took off our shoes and smashed the bottom of our feet with truncheons while some other coppers cuffed us behind the back. The police then returned their guns to the holsters.

"Levy what the fuck have those coppers just found in your car?" I asked him, as we were lying across the car bonnet with our heads twisted to the side.

"It's the black machine."

"What! You mean the black credit card machine that every one told you to leave in the hotel an hour ago?"

"Mmm," he nodded, realizing why he been told not to take it in the first place.

It wasn't even our fucking machine. Some prick gave it to him to see if he could get it fixed over here in Tenerife, and Now, because he'd kicked up such a fuss to us that he had to take it back to Gran Canaria to his Yugoslavian friend, he was given it back and had left the fucking thing underneath the passenger seat of a rental car that was basically classed as stolen! Not only that, but also a few minutes ago I'd got out of the car and was coaxed back in by the driver. He now had fucked off himself and left me in the shit with a credit card reader, a false credit card and his Hungarian friend who I had known for less than a fucking day.

I could feel the mobile vibrating in my pocket. The ringer had been set to escalate, which made the tone get louder on each ring. The boiler suited copper nearest to me looked over, tilted his head to the side then walked towards us. He pushed his hand into my tracksuit bottoms took out the now blurring phone and read out a number in Spanish.

"Nueve dos dos....."

The driver had slipped away through a few of the bars and had headed in the direction of our hotel as his was a taxi ride away in Los Cristianos. He ran into reception, pissing with sweat, and asked the receptionist which number suite the English were staying in. He entered the lift and reached the Royal suite room 501 Villa Cortes. He banged the door and rushed in explaining to Jamus, who had the hotel phone in his hand, what had happened.

"Don't tell me you've just called Shane from the hotel phone?" he asked.

"Yeah I have, I just wanted to know what was going on."

The door knocked......

IT'S ALL GONE PETE TONG

I was sitting on a low wooden bench with my back to the wall in a lime green painted room. A huge mirror like the ones that you see on TV when someone's interrogated stood in front of me. I hadn't seen where they had took Levy, and still wasn't quite sure what had happened exactly.

The shit that could come from all this could be a three-day bang up at the 'cop shop' and a release from the court on the third day or, up to our necks in it, and I mean thick sloppy stuff.

The door to my direct right opened. There were four, no five coppers staring at me all with truncheons being smacked in their hands.

Fucking hell,' I thought, if a take another battering after the war in Veronicas I'll probably end up dead. The one at the front of the group walked in and crouched down in front of me looking at my eyes. Someone had 'obviously' said something.

"Come with me," he said, lifting me up from the cuffs, which were still locked behind my back.

He led me through a series of passages, some of them I recognised from the ID parades that I'd been to just after my attack. We walked up a flight of stairs and into a room. Inside there was a table, with two chairs on both sides and a beige coloured push button telephone on top, which was off the hook. They uncuffed me.

"Sit there and co-operate," said another arriving officer, who promptly passed me the handset.

I frowned, and put it to my ear.

"Hello."

"Hello who is it?"

"Shane, its Jamus."

"Where the fuck are you?" I asked, very confused that he'd connected a call to me.

"I'm at the hotel," he replied, "The police want the key code to the safe in your room," he added.

I hesitated. "Where are the police now?"

"Standing next to me," he replied.

"Well what the fuck you doing calling me then?"

"They said that if you don't give it to them they're just gonna call reception anyway."

I now knew how deep the shit was!

The police had located the hotel by the phone call. 'Could the driver of the car have got away then?' I thought At this point I didn't know where he'd run to. A few minutes later, the Hungarian confirmed that the driver had also been nicked and was on the floor trying to blag an insulin attack. The police came to me and asked which type of insulin he took 'act rapid' or 'slow'. I told them I didn't know, either one of them could have put him in a coma shortly after.

While we were being strip searched and officially arrested, the two girls appeared. Emma, who was staying with Jamus and Tara who had flown over two days before to spend a little time with her sister. I just couldn't believe how all of these things could have happened in the sequence that they did.

We were registered and logged, fingerprints and all. The two girls moved away from us, and apparently were 'scared' into talking about something. They kept Jamus back at the hotel to answer questions about all of the equipment that had been found there. He denied any knowledge of ever seeing it before.

An hour later the undercover officer (MIP1) led me upstairs to a room with a table and three chairs.

"Sit," he said in a strong Spic accent.

The desk was covered with all the kit from the hotel. Sony Vaio laptops, magnetic stripe reader/writers and a single credit card with 'Wing hang bank' on the front. He picked up the laptop and shook it as you would a biscuit tin to see if there was anything inside. "All of the information is in here!"

I tilted my head back and frowned as if to say 'Yeah right.'

"You have a veeery veeery big problem. Every one at the hotel says that all of these things are for you! This portatil computer has inside all of the evidencia," he added, banging on the desk.

I started laughing and shrugged which seemed to make his blood boil a little.

"I haven't got a fucking clue what you're talking about. I don't give a toss what any one at the hotel said. You don't even know how to switch that computer on mate," I replied, as he placed the laptop back on the table.

After fiddling around with it for some time and realising what I'd said was true, 'he really couldn't switch it on' he closed the lid and pushed it away. "You will go to jail for a veeery veeery long time, and your friends will help."

"So where is Mr Olivetti now then?" I asked him.

He walked around the desk and smiled. "He is free,"

In the background, I could hear the faint sound of a voice in the background trying to get someone's attention. I recognised his voice straight away, it was Jamus.

So the bastards had nicked him as well and were trying to get more info from me by making out he had been freed.

"Ah, your Spanish policeman sounds English. I thought you said Olivetti was free. He sounds like he needs a piss to me?"

After a few minutes of trying his useless interrogation tactics, I was re-cuffed and escorted out of the room. We were six or seven steps from the bottom and the twat put his foot on my nice blue Armani shoes and pushed me. I tried to crouch low as possible to the ground so as not to take a big drop and managed to reach the bottom with just a few bruises. This prick on the street alone would have been destroyed in seconds. It was only the fact that he had an Englishman, with his hands cuffed behind his back who wasn't responding to his pathetic tactics that he could have done what he did. In the real world this boy was a nobody.

Eventually, Jamus came to the cells. He explained that when he was at the hotel the police had told him that if he helped them they would put a good word if for him with the judge. "I told them that the stuff wasn't mine and then the cunts arrested me," he laughed.

We had a very rough night as the heating in the cells was turned up high. We'd been given plastic mattresses which after a short while became sticky and uncomfortable and it was impossible for you to relax. We hadn't been given a drop of water in 20 hours and we were all dying of thirst and hunger to the extent of stomach cramps.

After more than a whole day without food or drink an officer turned up and gave us each a half a litre of warm water and some broken bread rolls that looked suspiciously like someones leftovers from the bin.

He opened my cell. "You can go to the toilet now if you want to. You will make declaration soon," he added.

I walked across the alleyway to the smelly, dirty toilet. It took me a while to go, but when I did, it came out a thick dark brown colour which told me my body was severely dehydrated.

We all agreed not to make any declarations until we went to court otherwise it would have given them more to fuck us with and make our bail difficult. Levente was opened up, escorted upstairs and gone for some time.

"What the fuck's your mate doing? He's been gone an hour and forty five minutes!" Just as I spoke, he returned.

Jay moved close to the bars. "Where you been Levy?"

"I had to make a declaration." He replied.

I banged on the bars. "WHAT! We fuckin' told you that no one was making a declaration. What the fuck did you say?"

He told us they'd asked him who he bought the car from and he told them he'd rented it from Neil Seddon 'cheap.' When they asked him who did the black machine for the credit cards belong to he said that he had never seen it in his life!

"I can't believe what I'm hearing Neil! Your friend, who along with you running away from the car, have just got us nicked, and he's now trying to put his machine on my toes!" I yelled.

"Fuckin' hell," said Jamus under his breath.

Neil Seddon was called next and while he'd gone I asked Jamus why he had called back from the hotel phone.

"My mobile had run out of credit and I wanted to know what was going on," he told me.

"But jay, didn't you realise that this would tell he police exactly where everything was?"

"I know, I know. I just didn't think it was so important at the time. My bird had just given me two lines of coke and a couple of Viagra. I wasn't thinking straight. We'll be OK I reckon if the rest of us don't make a declaration, they'll bail us from court and that'll be the end of it with a bit of luck."

Two hours later, Neil Seddon had not returned.

Some four hours on he arrived with a big smile on his face. We all smiled too. It was as if he'd got something good to tell us, but we later found out he'd been to the souvenir shop in Golf del Sur and pointed out to the police where a quantity of the cigarettes had been sold!

Jamus and I were asked to make declarations, but we both refused. What's the fucking point, the damage had all been done as far as I was concerned.

We made three appearances in the Instruction court during the four days torture we experienced in the police station. Mr Lawyer, Ruben Padron Perez, had been called at my request by one of the girls when they were released on the third day of our detention. He told me that the prosecutor was trying to press charges for Currency forgery and that the case was very serious.

It was 01:30am on august the 14th. The court had been trying to make sense of the goings on, but regardless of the fight Ruben had put up, they had decided that we should all go to prison on remand, awaiting trial.

"I'm very sorry Shane. I did everything possible. This judge has only been a judge for three months and she's scared to make a mistake and let anyone go," he told me sorrowfully.

"Ok Ruben thanks anyway."

"I shall apply for bail straight away ok"

"Ok thanks again," I thanked him, and off we went, 65 miles north to Centro Penitenciario Tenerife II in a small Guardia civil van, four up, hand cuffed behind the back and with no air conditioning.

THE DAY BEFORE JUDGEMENT DAY

Nearly three and a half years had passed us by before we received our day of trial. We'd been shipped back 300km south to Madrid's Valdemoro penitentiary for the third time in eighteen months.

The day before, my Madrid lawyer visited me at the prison and assured us that, taking into consideration the vast amount of remand we'd completed, it was a 'dead cert' that we'd be free sometime tomorrow.

"If the worst comes to the worst we can sign for the time that you've spent on remand and not go to trial. This means that you should automatically go free. If the judge doesn't agree to this then we go to trial. So don't you worry ok?" She stood up and adjusted her skirt. "They don't have enough to condemn you for false money," she waved and left as if it was all a pinch of salt.

JUDGEMENT DAY

We all sat chatting in a large communal cell underneath the Audiencia national in Madrid. I didn't feel the slightest bit nervous and found myself drifting away into thoughts of where I would be this time tomorrow.

Seddon's lawyer arrived and he was then taken from his cell to the communication section for a glass visit. A short time later Levente and I were called, then Jamus.

We were pushed into a tiny, pokey room, which was just wide enough for two people, and had to wait several minutes for the lawyer to appear.

"Right," she said, "We can do a deal with the prosecution and have the possibility to sign for 4 years for falsification of money and six months for fraud. It's the best we can do because the prosecutor has also sent a message to tell you that if you don't sign he will guarantee you 9 years!

I felt the colour drain from my face and looked at the big fellow. "Levy, I'm not signing for no fucking 4 years and seven months. She told us yesterday that we sign for the time spent on remand or, we go to trial . So were going to fucking trial, right?"

"Errrr er."

"Never mind fuckin' err. How can you change your mind so much since yesterday eh?" I snapped back.

The lawyer leant forward and put both of her hands on the desk in front of the glass. "Yes, I know Shane, but If you don't sign they will give you nine years for making the court go to the bother of calling the witnesses in Tenerife," she said nervously.

I too frowned and leant forwards. "What, so the witnesses aren't here or in Tenerife either? Then you must have done the fuckin' deal already. What do you think I am stupid?

"I know it must be difficult Shane, and it's not an easy decision to make, but it's the best I could do."

Seddon's lawyer appeared behind her. "Listen to me, you must sign or they'll give you a nine, ok!"

"Fuck you," I said, "you're only saying that because your client was the one with the credit card, which was in his own name. I personally had no credit cards or witnesses and I didn't 'bubble' half the shops up for receiving cigarettes with it. Now fuck off I'm talking to my lawyer, dick head!"

"The courts will never find you innocent now. You've been inside for three years. This is Spain, not England," he added.

"What, so you must think we asked to be on remand for three years? They put us here in the first place, and still, after all this time, you haven't even brought the fucking witnesses to trial…..What the fuck have we been paying you for?"

The thick metal doors behind us opened and Levente and I were both pulled-out. We were going to the court room now, one of the guards informed us as three others turned up to escort us all up in the elevator to the court level and into 'Sala numero uno.'

We were escorted through three short passageways and quite a narrow door, which led us into courtroom number one. We were not even given time to think about it. Two police officers were seated one either side of us with pistols. I made the lawyers very nervous as I repeatedly told everyone 'I wasn't going to sign!'

My lawyer, who had given it the 'Big un" with us the day before at the prison, turned pale in the face and resembled a mouse, dwarfed by the powers that surrounded her.

The judge banged the hammer and ordered that the trial begin.

"All of the people are here today for a presumed crime of Falsification of Currency, Fraud and International Organised Crime. You all have the option to plead guilty and receive four years falsification and six months for fraud. If one of the four people here today doesn't sign then 'all' of you shall go to trial," she added. "Neil Seddon, do you plead guilty or not guilty?"

"Guilty."

"Shane Lloyd, do you plead guilty or not guilty?"

I didn't answer and the other three all looked round at me.

"Im not fucking signing, we'll fight like we've been saying for the past three years!"

Jamus rubbed his forehead. "I know what you mean Shane, but what about if they give us a niner?"

"They're going to fuck us up if we don't," added Levy.

I looked up to the lawyer for help, and caught a quick glimpse of her terrified face. She then turned away and all I could see was the back of her head. The police officer who was sitting to my right nudged me and told me to be quiet as I started ranting onto the others.

"You fucking shut up cunt face," I told him, boiling with temper.

If one of us didn't sign then, all four of us would have to go to trial so in that case I'd been backed in to a corner. I couldn't risk going to trial, being released and leaving the rest of them with a niner, even if I wasn't happy about some of the things that'd been done. I jumped out of my chair.

"I'm only signing for these three!" I screamed!!!

"Mr Lloyd," said the judge, "That is not the answer to the question we asked you. Are you Guilty, or not guilty?"

"Guilty," I replied, as I sat down absolutely gutted, giving in to the pre-arranged slaughtering.

We were all asked to sign hand written documents, and that was it!

Before we knew it, we were on our way back to Valdemoro. It was a very strange feeling, as if it hadn't really happened.

Three weeks later, I received my sentence from the 'Gente judicial.'

"Senor Lloyd, I have to first of all read to you what it is you have exactly done in this case, and then you have to sign the document," she said.

After five or so minutes of scanning the four-page document several times, she looked up at me. "Mmm, it doesn't actually say what it was that you did. All I can tell you is that your sentence is four years and seven months. Just sign there Mr Lloyd, please."

I returned some few weeks later back on the gruesome 300-kilometre ride to Valladolid.

On entry, the screws greeted me. "Ah inglish, back again are we?"

I didn't even bother to answer them, and after explaining to everyone repetitively what had happened in court I sat up against the wall on the floor in the concrete yard on a piece of cardboard with my mates Russian, Oleg Svelik and a Moroccan lad called Adil Kouara and smoked a huge spliff

The next day I made a formal request to the Director of the prison to complete the rest my sentence in England.

I received confirmation from the 'Spanish' Ministry of Justice that on Fourth of July (Independence Day!) my request for repatriation was granted.

It was going to take around twelve months they told me.

On the 21st of August 2007, Shane Lloyd was 'finally' repatriated from Madrid in Spain. The British authorities interviewed him about the entire 'goings on' and after spending a few months in HMP Wandsworth; he was then transferred to HMP Standford Hill open prison on the Isle of Sheppey near Kent.

Even though he had been on remand for three years and paid nearly 5years of his sentence. They gave him no parole or remission for the time spent in Spain. His release date was the 3rd of January 2008. He now pursues a 'Drug and Alcohol free' life as a writer and inventor.

Smile and Be Happy

Champers xxx

Look out for 'Champers' the film!

SHOUTS

John, Julie and kids, Liggo, Max and family, The Meacham's, The Lloyds, Steve and Greg Pettitt, Deb, Emma, Steven, Brandon & Harrison Pettitt, Scott N & Family, Groove, Ron & Julie, Mackie, Mick, Tonna, Zac, Shamus, Fletch, Stu, Darren, Craig, MJ, Mark, Graham, Lisa, Owen Strickland, Derek the dancing doorman, Loza, Scott, Scott M, Arthur, Louise, Heidi, Tracy Nicholas, Sarah, Natalie, H, Debbie, Paul, Lisa, Robo, Big Jim, Chrissie Phipps, Heidi, Sten, Neil Jackson(Beacon Radio),Emily, Natalie and Darren Davis, Justin, Evo, Rocket Ron, Gerard, Gary Baker, Paul Arbor, Dj Shane (Galaxy FM), Clinton, Graham, DJ jack, Kish, Big Colin, H, Mark, Nick the DJ, Paul Jones, Michael "Scissorhands" Kingston, Vanessa, Pigeon, Lorraine Porter, Tony Brookes, Sweaty, Hagga, Sharon O'Grady, Debbie, Stevie, John, Dave, Christian, Butch, and Daniel Broadhurst, Booey, The Perv, Roy O'Grady, Spen, Andrew O'Grady, Mel, Theresa, Sue, Leanne, all of the Walsall university students of '98', Governor and Ben the guard dogs.

Hort, Julie, Paul Hickenbottom, Freddy, Julie & Oggy, Tracy, Jodie, Kayleigh, Wendy, Jim and Lotty, Az,Jase, Jd, Stan. The Johnsons: - Lee, Neil, Choch, Wolfy, Gemma, Ellen & Shaun, Katie & Gunter, Susan, Luke, Jean & Graham. Dan, Flump, Carl, Brett, Lee & Woza Kent, Stu,Coop, Noggin, Damien, Shane, H, Ninny, Azum, , T, Wendy, Julie, Mel, Dalton and family, Malcolm Sanders, Ann Poxen, Shaun Gun, Banger, Craddock, Frog, Jane, Craddock, Shaun, Steve Morrel, Brooko, Kirky, Doza, Scarlet, Aza, Grant Talbot, Ian and Phil Parry, Neil and Mark Chapman, Polly, Big Neil, Elvis, Nobby and family, Doug, Darren Winters, Bret, Gary Lawton, Col the Medic, Scot, Tracy, Fear not, Biker Dave and the boys, 'The Italians' Carlo and Gino, All of the Sundiessential and 'Tin Tins' crew of '96' **Lucy Kinchin Jade**

Bishop Owen Strickland Kelly Evison Julie Gleeson Craig Walters

Champagne Shane Shane Lloyd Chris Kinchin Giles Johnston Rude Stu Beauchamp Vicky Bradbury Karla Louise Russon John Hammond House Proud Presents Debby Smith Anne Marie Weir Bellavista Cairns

Melissa Lesley Gibb Julie Anne Fox Peter Hansell Charlie Roberts Stephen Thompson Rachel Victoria Dewar Beverley Larke Charlotte Malcolm Nasrine Chérry Vanessa Scott Kae Bloor Gail Lote Rachael Melia-Scott Tracey Lloyd Hayley Louise Kara Minter Hayley Phipps Mark Gibbs Angela Pappin-Cole Daniel Pietro Baker

Trish Park Catherine Murphy Mark Freeman Dan Leach Brittany Gunter Pauline Bowler James Michael Quilliam Andrew Mcgarvey Stuart Barnett Shirley Sujanani Andrew Canadine Jane Hill Sienna Davids

Wayne Michael Haskett Natale Haydon-davis Kayleigh Louise Harrison Stacey Griffiths Vicki Clacken Emma Beach Jay Wesson Rachael Kelly Jodie Walls James Stanley 'Sophie Bladen Vanessa Bellini Charlotte Brazier Sandra Tocilla Matt Jukes Zane Hoddle Lyons Nikki Morris Emily Vincent Darren Davis Michaela Murphy

Hollie-may Kelly Carly Smithson Amy Meek Vicki Welsh Jai Small Eliz Laura Potts Becky Dolphin

Nikkita Nicolson Nicola Coxon Richard Stinson Ben Sparey Kelly Greenfield Sophie Grime Kerry Condron

Jason Yorke Michael Anthony Marshall Steve Langston Jamie Owens Roya Mesbah

Stephen DjSteveewonder Reynolds George Clifton Rebecca Smith Mel Michael Gemma Lewis Joanne Archer

Julie Burns Emma Jae Gardner Kelly Arbuckle Ross Taylor Lee Marshall Clare Parsonage Suzanne Howe

Neil Martin Johnson Emma L Sutton Michelle Teresa Mason Danielle Jade Peachy Skett Andrew Stuart Peel

Mark Moore Paul Anthony Johnson Amy Lawrence Emma Brendon Platter Claire Weston Hamilton

Leah Crag-chaderton Katie Louise Chapman Sally Wise Emma Sherriff Jodie Hickinbottom Larissa Welborn

Tom Dalloway Greg Pettitt Michelle Russell Dean Smith Karen

Gooch Laura Kind Danny Small Anna Willis

Luke Samo Sampson Jill Carman Hazel D-p Glen Noad Emma Bilsland Mark Freeman Kenny J. M Rodriguez Angela Griffiths Was Spooner Melvyn Mansell Hannah Lucas Helen Hanson Jane Mason Paula Gerrard Lord David Stephen Fullerton Ralph Jones Raquel Shaw Djahmed Abd Elrauof Jane Fellows Jenny Channell Colette Talbot Michael Wall Tanya O'grady Kelly Chandler Tina Mansell Samantha Morris Lincoln Hunt

Annabelle PrincessConsuella Lancaster Kate Horton Suzanne Dolphin Tamra Forde Karen Murphy Matt Lowe Jacqueline Turner Paul Willetts Rogers James Harrison Pettitt Brandon Pettitt Matt Lewis Suzanne Treble

Heidi Readman-ahmed Roger Foster Bernice Haycock Neil Alexander Jamison Jamus Oliveti Emily Dalloway

Robbie Smith Nathan Kelly Luke Cain Kirk Mcroberts Katie Parry Laura Whitehouse Leanne Winsper

Amanda Vaughan Graham Pinches Libby Flenley James O'grady Stephanie Levy Carl Dowd-Mackenzie

Sarah Morris Rob Aston Bev Merriman Lizzie Ann Clutterbuck Allana Silk Dj Kideva Elaine Hickinbottom Charlotte Johnston Dianne Metcalfe-Pilkington Sam Perry Jade Russell Gareth John Ralph Kenny Solomon

Stuart Mckie Nick Parkinson Shane Horney Sarah-Jane Mawdsley Matt Rochelle Wolfy Johnson Mathew Kind

Paul Dolphin Katie Jayne Buckle Nigel Thomas Kim Phan Diane Davies Lorraine Cook Scot Miles Scott Walker James Foggon Kerry Freeman Christine Berrisford Carina Affeldt Vicky Smith Steve O Toole

Scott 'Superyam' Merrett Rob 'Doc' Taylor Donna Phillips Maxine Ryan Adele-Louise Preggers Leighton

Katie Hayward Jack Keen Mark Chapman Clint Hartland Ashley Leech Ryan Leach Michela Garbi Patrick Swayze Lloyd Claire Franey Dani Liggins Neil Wright Pam Cole Kerry Baugh Richard Chapman Shane Knowles

Debz Edmondson Toni Russell Gerard Kelly Stuart Morton Richard Senior Marta Perez Martina Skowronska

Kev Thorne Leanne Sansom Zowie Evans Steven Pettitt Ruth

Brook Sophie Madhead Freeman Assum Khan Andy McLaren Kelly Lowe Sharon O'grady,

TENERIFE

Matt, Kelly and family, Naughty Neil, Steve ,JD, Giles, Jordie, Paddy, Jane, Jordie John, Lucinda ,Ginger George, Greg, Paddy, Graham, Conner, Shabba, Mario, Marco, Karen, Ross, Claire, Big Shane and Dave, Janis, Emma, Bernie, Shelly, Kelly, Mitch, Stan, Katie 1, Katie 2,Zoe, Joe, Ashley, Mark, Joelean, Pat and Nobby, Moroccan Sammy, Danny, Fernando, DJ Tiny, DJ Alex and all of the Veronicas and Starco street 'Chingers' from '97' to 2001, Russian Alex, The Scoucers, Big Michael Landel, Linzie dawn Mackenzie, Emma and Tara Marshal, Suzie Wilden, Terry Coldwell and Brian Harvey (East 17), Rachel (S Club 7), Lenny Henry, Big Frank Bruno, Prince Nazeem, Robbie Williams, Big Joe Egan &Anita Dobson (Angie from East enders)

C.P. (Centro penitentiary) Spain & Canary Islands

Mr. Peter Hans, Jose Barrios, Danny O'Connell, Norma Martindale, Tony Ike Chuku, Kopovich, Chris and Gary, Oleg Svedlek, Adil Kouara, Christian Anderson, Brother, Mohammed Snaufee, Mauricio 'Zemmen Boy' Rubio, Jesus Martinez, Mr. Fred Silas, The Russian crew, The Romanians, The Sicily crew, KK, Juan, Davuk, Stefanov, Abdullah, MWS, Markus Smidt, Michael Marx,

H.M.P. (Her majesty's prisons)

Pat Windgrove, Pat, Glen Harris, Eddie, John Mathews, John (Essex), Mo, Richard Watson, Peter, Bhav Rana, Tony Wood, Colin Lawrence, Johnny Alder, Matt bishop,

ALL MY FRIENDS AND ASSOCIATES.

About the Author

A happy go lucky kid who fought his way life with a smile an an adventurous imagination. Wherever there was chaos you could usually find him in the middle of it. He worked most of his life in Clubs and bar's in the West midlands and surrounding area's up untill the mid ninties where he moved to the Canary Islands to open his own nightclub 'Casa Loca' in Playa de Las Americas, Tenerife.

'There's never a dull moment when he's around!'

CPSIA information can be obtained at www.ICGtesting.com
Printed in the USA
LVOW071729220313

325639LV00001B/292/P